Abandoned but Not Crushed
...And Finding Joy Again

By Casey Powell

Creative Force Press

Christie,
Thank you so much
for all of your advice!
Hope you enjoy my book!

Creative Force Press

Abandoned but Not Crushed
© 2018 by Casey Powell
www.CaseyPowellAuthor.com

This title is also available as an eBook. Visit
www.CreativeForcePress.com/titles for more information.

Published by Creative Force Press
4704 Pacific Ave, Suite C, Lacey, WA 98503
www.CreativeForcePress.com

ISBN: 978-1-939989-31-4

Printed in the United States of America
Cover Photos © Reese's Photography

To my parents,
thank you for your love and guidance!

To my children, my hope is for each of you to
lean on God for EVERYTHING, now and forever!

"I can do all things through Christ who strengthens me."
Philippians 4:13

Table of Contents

Note to Readers

This is a true story

I have done my best to tell this story 100% accurately and faithfully, with no embellishment and with the benefit of having spent several years overcoming the intense emotions I felt when these events were taking place.

However, many of the players in this drama are still living. I respect their privacy, and I wouldn't want to hurt any of them. As you will see, some of these people are the sort of folks who have no scruples about suing a grieving widow and single mother regardless of the truth of her story. Accordingly, and upon the advice of legal counsel, I have changed many names as well as the name of the company my late husband and I owned and operated.

Having said that, I do not apologize for anything I have written here. These were my experiences. The truth matters, and this story needed to be told.

Chapter 1

Our Fairytale Love Story

I had what seemed to be a fairytale marriage, a caring father to my children, a beautiful new home on a golf course and a wonderful, loving extended family. Then came the knock on my door that cold January morning, delivering the worst news that forever changed my life.

The Blind Date

Chris and I met on a blind date in January, 2003. As you all know, the possibility of a blind date going well is extremely low. I'd been on one blind date prior to this one and it wasn't so good, but I was more optimistic this time around. Chris's high school best-friend, Jared, was dating my college roommate, Tessa, and they thought we should meet. I trusted my roommate's judgement because she was a good girl, so I valued her opinion. Tessa could light up a room with her smile alone. She was a sweet southern girl, raised in a strong Christian home. I lived with Tessa long enough to know that she valued relationships and her faith more than anything else. I didn't agree to the blind date until I evaluated the background information on this guy. Tessa said he came from a Baptist family and his grandfather was a Baptist minister. Chris was a semi-professional soccer player in his late teens and he was currently working as the General Manager for the Golden Knights, a minor-league hockey team in Florida. The sports fan that I am perked up at the sound of that. An athlete, and a General Manager for a sports team, hmmm...*I'm in*! I grew up playing sports and watching sports, so a man with his history and current occupation sounded intriguing. Then, I learned he was recently divorced and wasn't sure how to process that piece of information. He was only married for a little over a year. Everything else about him sounded wonderful, so I decided to meet him.

Our first date was a group date. Joining us were my sister and brother-in-law, Rene and Tom, and my roommate Tessa and her boyfriend, Jared. We decided to meet in the middle since they were staying in Chicago and we were two hours south in Central Illinois. We met at a Red Lobster. The three of us arrived before the others and I was a nervous wreck. The anticipation was wearing me out! Out of the corner of my eye I saw them walk in. When I first laid eyes on Chris, I thought, *this might be a good thing*. He was tall, lean, handsome, had dark hair, crystal blue eyes, and a charming smile. He was wearing a black leather jacket, button down shirt, jeans and dress shoes.

Conversation was so easy around that table. He seemed fun and very witty. He was a conversation starter for sure. He didn't have an ounce of shyness from what I gathered, and even my brother-in-law approved. Having the thumbs-up confirmation from family was crucial.

After dinner, he gave me his phone number on a napkin. I remember it was written with purple ink; purple because that was the only pen I had in my purse. These were the days without smart phones – just dumb flip phones with no way to easily capture someone's number or text. We called each other and spoke on the phone later that night.

Chris lived in Florida and had flown in for a Chicago Blackhawks game and a quick visit with friends, so he planned to fly back home the very next day. I told my sister and brother-in-law on the drive home that I thought he was "the one!" I never believed in love at first site, but Chris was so striking and hit all the high points: fun to talk to, came from a great family, had a good job and was a Christian. Sharing the same beliefs, or similar beliefs was very important to me. We dated long distance for a few months, flying back and forth to see each other. It was obvious where this was headed. On one visit, I flew down to see him and he planned a fantastically romantic night on the beach to wine and dine me. We cruised the Florida coast with the convertible top down, enjoying the view and the warm air. He really knew how to make a girl feel special. *Finally after years of the dating, I think I'm done.* He was different than anyone else I'd ever met. He was mature, responsible and ambitious.

Another time I flew down to see Chris, he told me prior to the trip that we were meeting the Golden Knights' coach and his wife for dinner along with some other staff. I wasn't up to speed with the National Hockey League, so I didn't know a thing about teams and statistics. When Chris mentioned the head coach's name, Ron Duguay, it didn't ring a bell with me. Little did I know that Ron was a retired Canadian professional hockey player and coach who played 12 seasons in the National Hockey League, playing for teams such as the New York Rangers and Detroit Red Wings. Chris mentioned Ron's wife, Kim Alexis, will be joining him also. *Wait, Kim Alexis the super model?* She was a former fashion model in the 1980's that landed more than 500 magazine covers. Now Chris had my attention. I was anxious to meet Kim Alexis.

We arrived at the restaurant and I was seated right next to Kim. She was beautiful. Of course she was! She was a famous model and actress I learned. Sitting next to Kim Alexis, engaging in hilarious conversation, sharing a seaweed appetizer with her, was the last thing I ever saw myself doing. She told us this funny story about being in the backyard with her children and killing a snake. Out of all things, a former fashion model kills a snake. That dinner was one of the most memorable dinners in my life.

After those few months of long distance dating, Chris decided to move up to Illinois to job search there. He moved to Illinois in June of 2003. As I look back I think "it sure would have been wise to have had a job *before* moving. He rented a nice apartment in town and my family helped him move in. After a couple of weeks of job searching, my Dad mentioned to Chris that he should come work for him at Midwestern Repair and Maintenance Service.

My parents owned and operated a successful commercial repair business, Midwestern Repair and Maintenance Service, for 30 years. My Dad was a well-respected expert in his field and one of the only few in the area. His work was perfection. He always said, "Don't do the job if it's not going to be done right." My Dad was also well-known for his confident approach when asking someone if they knew if they were going to heaven. Depending on their answer, that would lead to the next question about Christianity and Jesus Christ. My Dad is very good at explaining what faith is. I chuckle at him. I never had the audacity to ask the things my dad asks. He's a brave man, always up for a challenge.

Chris was hired to help manage the business and take some of the workload off my father. I had worked for my Dad since I was very young, so I was looking forward to Chris being a part of the family business, too. At that time though, I had been happily employed at a sports and fitness publishing company for three years. I started as a Production Assistant, quickly moving my way up to Academic Production Manager. My job consisted of managing the production of academic books from the time they were acquired from the author, to having the final printed book in hand. I worked directly with the editorial staff, art and photo departments and the graphic design team. I was also solely responsible for quoting the books with printers all over the United States and overseas. The corporate world was enjoyable and I figured I'd work up until retirement in it.

Small-town living didn't seem to bother Chris at all. He was a social guy and very approachable. He adjusted well in my hometown of 5500 people. He attended church with my family and I every Sunday, and I was starting to see how he was going to fit in perfectly.

One July afternoon, I stopped by his apartment before we headed out to a family gathering. He was sitting on the couch and I stood there and said, "Okay, let's get going." He said, "Hey, first can you go get me a Kleenex please?" So I went into the restroom to grab a tissue for him, and sitting inside the opening of the tissue box was a jewelry box. *A ring box?!* I grabbed it, walked back into the living room and said, "Chris, what is this?", "What? Come here, I can't see it" he said, innocently. As I got closer to him, he dropped down on one knee and popped the question. Of course I said yes. Even though we only knew each other for four months, I knew he was Mr. Right from the night of our blind date. At the age of 24, I never felt so certain about someone in my life and I was elated to be his wife!

A few months after the proposal, we took a trip to Florida to visit Chris's family. I figured over the course of 7 months I had learned everything about Chris that I wanted to know. Getting to know someone takes time, but since we had an express relationship, asking questions about major topics was something I had to do right away. During that visit in Florida, I learned something about Chris that he never told me before. I was enjoying the afternoon with a close relative of his, when the topic of Chris's bankruptcy came up. I said "Bankruptcy, what bankruptcy?" Chris never mentioned this to me. This news was alarming. When you think of a bankruptcy, you think of someone having serious money problems. His bankruptcy occurred while in college, more than six years prior. When I heard this news I was upset but didn't outwardly show it. *How will I address this with Chris?* I tried telling myself, *it happened over six years ago, it's fine.* Then I thought, *what if there is something else I don't know about?*

That very next day Chris and I went to dinner on the beach. As I was sitting across the table from him I was stressing about how to address the bankruptcy topic. Was I making a bigger deal out of it then it needed to be? Without any further hesitation, I blurted out, "Hey, what's this about your bankruptcy back in college?" "Oh," he replied. "I had a rough first year in school and traveling around with soccer." He acted like it was a typical young college kid mistake. Nothing alarmed me about Chris before this conversation, so I decided to believe him and drop the subject.

The Wedding and the Honeymoon

I couldn't believe I was engaged. My family seemed to like him and everyone was so happy for us. We started to plan the wedding and decided May 29th would be the date – ten good months to pull together the most beautiful dream wedding ever. As a young girl, I would sketch pictures of ball gown dresses and knew someday I'd wear one for my wedding. I even dressed my Barbie dolls in gorgeous ball gowns. In my mind, every girl's dream was to feel like a princess on her wedding day.

The perfect dress was found! It was a stunning, stark white, strapless ball gown with crystal beading around the torso and a blossoming tulle skirt. It was everything I ever dreamed of for my wedding day. Choosing the bridesmaid dresses wasn't as easy. Selecting our wedding colors took a lot of thought. We decided on periwinkle, a purple-blue color like that of a periwinkle flower. All of my bridesmaids could wear that color well. Everything was coming together: the venue, the décor, music, food, bridal showers, and the bachelorette party. Ten months flew by in a flash.

During those months, Chris and I purchased a perfect starter house, known as the "4th Street" house. We bought the two-story home as a renovation project. It is best described as a traditional cottage home with a detached garage. This house had potential to have magnificent curb appeal. We worked night and day on that house on 4th Street, along with our wedding planning, and miraculously had it move-in ready by our wedding date.

We were married in May 2004. We had a beautiful wedding at my church in our hometown. We had around 230 guests attend. I grew up in the Bible Church previously located across town before it expanded, then it moved to the new location where we were married. For 24 years straight I attended Bible Church every Sunday unless we were on vacation. Attending meant we were there for Sunday morning Sunday school class at 9:00 a.m., the sermon at 10:20 a.m. and Sunday evening service at 6:30. On Wednesdays, my sister and I participated in the youth programs all the way through high school. Every summer we attended a week of vacation Bible school through eighth grade. We also attended most of the church potlucks there as well. Potlucks were *the thing* back in the 1980s! Everyone brought a dish to the church to celebrate something or just to have a lunch with church family. It was a great time of fellowship and of course, as kids, we loved to run around and play.

The church where I attended from the week I was born until 2003 when the new church building went up across town

The new Bible Church building where we were married

Once the wedding ceremony and photography session was over, that meant party time! An extended Cadillac Escalade limousine waited outside the church for the bridal party – our elegant shuttle to the reception, which was 45 minutes away. To this day, we still talk about that limo ride. It was like a night club on wheels, fully stocked with drinks, rotating light show and the best throwback music ever written. Great memories were made on that 45-minute ride to the reception.

My parents gave us the most alluring golf course wedding reception. The setting was perfect! In May, you are lucky to get a warm sunny day in our area. The photographers directed us to the fairways and greens for some stunning outdoor photos. They even captured some beautiful photos in the tall prairie grass. The venue met all of my expectations. From the enticing three-tiered ice sculpture to the exquisite, eye-catching floral centerpieces, it was everything I had dreamed of for my wedding day. The music, family and friends, food, cocktails and best of all, I was married to Mr. Right!

The following morning, we had to load up and head home for the gift-opening gathering with family. Weddings in my family are a weekend event! After all the gifts were opened, we packed up and headed to the airport for the start of our honeymoon.

That weekend we traveled to Maui for our honeymoon. The five-hour flight was a little long, but we were starting our life together on that flight. Everything was exciting and new. Chris was such a gentleman and he made the trip fun. He was used to traveling the world as a semi-pro soccer player and he always enjoyed traveling for leisure as well.

We landed in Maui and as we walked off the plane, we heard "Aloha" as they welcomed us with beautiful purple and white plumeria-flowered leis. It was just like the movies. When we arrived at the resort to check in, they also gave us a lei, except it was one with tropical beads. I felt like a celebrity. The resort was absolutely gorgeous. The lobby area included an open-air tropical garden, with peek-a-boo views of the turquoise ocean. Birds were chirping, waterfalls were bubbling all throughout the lobby. I'd never seen anything like it before. Growing up family vacations consisted mostly of road trips: from the Rocky Mountains, Grand Canyon, a Dude ranch in Wyoming, fishing trip to Canada, road trips to Texas, Arizona, New Mexico, California, once to Washington D.C., etc. Never to any warm beaches near the equator. We vacationed in the 90's built Ford Conversion van with the extremely comfortable third row couch that folded down into a bed. The van also housed a television with a VHS player. This 11 mile per gallon van was the most popular dream ride for any road trip. In my late teens after graduation, my best friend, Shelly, and I started our own adventures to Myrtle Beach, South Carolina, Ft. Lauderdale, Florida, and Dallas, Texas. Instead of spending long hours in a car, we called American Airlines. We were young and free and ready to live it up after high school graduation!

Throughout the honeymoon we drove along the coast in a convertible and enjoyed the beautiful Hawaiian scenery. We visited a state park to experience the beauty of Maui, enjoyed the Bubba Gump restaurant and shopped at the beachside stores. It was the most romantic vacation I've ever been on. I was only 25 and never before experienced a 5-star beach resort with more than one restaurant to choose from. I couldn't wait to plan our next trip!

Life as a newlywed was so new to me. We didn't live together until after we were married, which is so different than how society does things anymore. I was raised with strong beliefs about dating and marriage. My parents instilled good morals in us at a very young age. When I knew Chris was the right man for me, I made the decision to follow what scripture says.

We adapted well to married life and knew what was next to come. Not too long after we got married we decided to try for a baby. We both thought, why wait? I always thought getting pregnant would be easy. I was young and naïve. It took several months, but finally we had good news to tell everyone. The following Christmas, we announced our joyful news: we were expecting our first baby in August of 2005. Not only did my family have our pregnancy to celebrate, but two pregnancies! Soon after we announced our good news, my cousin Tara and her husband, Wes, announced they were expecting also! Our due dates were only one week apart. Experiencing pregnancy for the first time was a whole new world. Having my cousin to walk through it with me made the experience even better. Tara and I grew up very close. We were only one year apart in age and were always more like sisters and best friends. Our mothers were only five years apart in age, and we all lived within a few blocks of each other.

For the entire nine months of pregnancy we were in

the process of building a new house. It wasn't quite finished yet, and since we had already sold our 4th Street cottage home, we were living with family until we could move in. Chris and I were both anxious for the arrival of our baby girl and we wanted everything to be perfect for her in our new home.

Our precious little girl, Kristin, was born in August. Chris bonded with her right away. Seeing him hold his little girl was the most precious sight. She was six weeks old when it was time to move in to our new home. My husband was the general contractor on the home and did a great job making the home perfect. We were excited to start our new life there as a family of three. We painted her nursery a solid bright pink on two of the walls, and pink and white stripes on the other two walls. Her room had a white crib with a matching armoire and changing table. It was picture perfect!

Being a parent was very new to both of us, but Chris always had a way of making things feel okay. He was always a comforting presence in new situations.

Chapter 2

Business Decisions

In the spring of 2007, Chris approached me with the idea of purchasing my parents' company, Midwestern Repair and Maintenance Service (Midwestern). I thought it was a great idea...if we could afford it. Growing up, I imagined I would be me running my Dad's company someday, but having a husband with that desire was even better. I was a daddy's girl at a very young age and had worked for my Dad since age 12. My job started out in the shop of course, then I graduated to running a winch lines and other equipment. I was a 16-year-old girl wearing a hard hat and work boots, operating the ditch witch, driving a one-ton dually truck pulling an 18 ft trailer and more. I did everything from detailing work trucks, to administrative work, to going on the job sites with the crews. I even spent my college internship there doing administrative work with the office staff. I always saw myself being a part of Midwestern, so I was thrilled at the idea of taking ownership with my husband.

We purchased Midwestern Repair and Maintenance Service in 2007 and our first son was born a few months later. Life was grand! I had the perfect job working at a publishing company, I had two beautiful children and a wonderful husband. I really loved my job at the publishing company and imagined myself retiring from there. Although once I experienced being a mom, my thoughts shifted a little. I knew I wasn't cut out to be a full-time stay-at-home mom, but I wanted more flexibility to be with my children. I approached Chris with my idea of opening a fitness business. After weeks of discussion, Chris agreed we should move forward with the idea. My dream of running a fitness club in my hometown was fulfilled.

Growing up, I had multiple conversations with my dad about Forest Grove needing a gym. I can remember being 14, just a freshman in high school, feeling intrigued by exercise and fitness. Sports were a big part of my life: softball, volleyball, basketball and track. In my free time, I would use the home treadmill in our downstairs room. I would turn on the small box-television on a shelf directly in front of the treadmill and walk for minutes or sometimes hours. It wasn't about losing weight at that point. This was an era where Jane Fonda's videos were popular and "Buns of Steel" exercise videos were a hit! I was interested in how the body could be transformed with exercise and dedication. This era was more of a man's world for weight lifting. It wasn't common for women to lift weights in the 80's and 90's. Commercial gyms were hard to come by and fitness was just hitting the market. Jane Fonda did a pretty good job influencing women to start getting fit.

Soon after we made the decision to plan for the fitness club, I learned about a couple in my hometown who also wanted to open a gym. I had attended their wedding 12 years prior, so I knew them very well. When you come from a small town of under 5500 people, word travels fast. In some cases that can be a great thing!

I decided to give them a call so we could explore the idea of co-owning. We met and discussed a business plan and agreed to start a fitness club together: Canton Fitness Club. I was on cloud nine! My passion for health and fitness finally led me to have a gym of my own.

The four of us immediately started looking at real estate in town. We ended up finding a large, 5000 square foot Morton building on the main street in town. The building sat on a corner lot on a high traffic road. When you think of opening a business, location is a major aspect to consider. After purchasing the building, we started the remodeling project right away.

In the fall of 2008 we opened the fitness club. The gym had roughly 3000 square feet of open space. We filled up that space with cardio and weight machines. In the back corner of the gym, we created an 800 square foot studio where the group fitness classes would be held. Towards the front corner of the gym was a playroom. As parents of young children ourselves, we knew how difficult it is to find time to workout. We filled that room with toys, books, coloring books and crayons, and we even had the Disney Channel playing on a wall-mounted television. It was a dream room for kids!

A couple of years went by and business was going well. I was working at the gym throughout the week teaching fitness classes and started doing personal training. Chris was busy running a successful business.

One day Chris approached me with the idea of a couple friends, Zach and Betsy, investing in the family business. I thought partnering up with them in this journey sounded great. I had known Betsy since we were young kids and I'd known Zach since high school. Betsy and my sister, Rene, had been best friends growing up. Betsy was a country girl with a farm full of animals. My sister and I were small town city girls. In our later years, Betsy and I became closer because we had a lot in common and our husbands were golfing buddies.

Chris decided to call a meeting so the four of us could discuss a business plan. We were all looking forward to this new endeavor! We knew the men would be working at the company while the women handled our other professions. After some discussion and planning, it was settled. Zach and Betsy were to become our Midwestern Repair and Maintenance Service partners.

Later that year, Betsy and I both found out we were pregnant and our due dates were only a month a part. It was so fun going through the pregnancy with a friend. We shared the experience together, venting about all the aches and pains and planning for our newborns. It was very exciting!

Chris and Zach were busy running Midwestern and I was busy working at my gym, being a mom, and preparing for our third child, a second little girl, due in the winter of 2010.

Gambling Hobby

I specifically remember every football season was the highlight of the year. Chris enjoyed placing a $50 or $100 dollar bet on games here and there. He wouldn't hide it from me, or so I thought, so I was okay with what he was doing. Plus, we didn't have joint bank accounts, so if he lost a couple games, I wasn't aware of his checks and balances. I believed he was smart enough to know when enough was enough and never was the type of wife to tell him what to do.

We had a lot going on. We weren't exactly the *Leave It to Beaver* family. Both of us were busy working parents. Two businesses, three small children, our oldest daughter in competitive travel dance. You could say 2010 was all about adjusting to our new (crazy) normal.

I struggled with post-partum depression after my third pregnancy, and some of you may know about having a baby in the winter and how post-partum can seem a whole lot worse. It was a long winter and our second child was almost a one-year-old. For some reason I couldn't shake the somberness. I was more down than normal. Chris seemed consumed in his Blackberry, busy with work I assumed. He was quiet and more distant.

For months he had been telling me things about my dad that I *never* thought sounded like something my dad would do or say. He was becoming very negative about my parents. I just thought he was frustrated because he was stressed with running the business. He never experienced the blood, sweat and tears my parents went through growing that business for the first 30 years. So, at times I wasn't sure if I was struggling with post-partum or just was sad and confused by all the negative words I was listening to about my father, who I looked up to my entire life. The harsh words bothered me to the point

24

where I had to call my mom and inform her of what Chris was telling me. My mom didn't seem to be worried much because it didn't sound like something my dad would do, yet Chris had me convinced.

My dad is a workaholic, perfectionist, loyal and the most generous Christian man you will ever know! He spent most of his career traveling 5-6 days a week, being home on Sundays for church. My sister and I were used to our dad traveling to jobs while mom held down the fort at home. It wasn't unusual for me to be living the same married life my mom experienced. My dad's employees would tell me my dad would loan them money if they were short. He was also the type to get distracted easily and offer a hand when needed. He has a servant's heart.

One day an older gentleman came into my gym to inquire about membership. He said, "If you are even 10% the person your dad is, then you are doing okay." I thought that was sweet considering it was the first time I'd met this farmer, but he knew my dad. I had the kind of parents that were always involved in the church and things in the community. My mom was (and still is) in the choir, on the praise team, and also taught Sunday school. My Dad was a deacon, serving on the Benevolence committee for years, and he was very active on the Missions committee. The Benevolence committee is primarily responsible for studying the needs of the church families and other persons in the community. My dad is a very compassionate person who strives to help wherever he can. He's attended numerous missions trips all over the world: Aguascalientes, Mexico four times, France,

Burkina Faso, Zimbabwe, Haiti, the Philippines twice, Vancouver Island BC Canada eight times, and Israel. You could say he's a world traveler. This is who I knew my dad to be.

The evenings at home with Chris and the kids seemed as normal as could be. We appeared to be living the dream. Precious little kids can seem to bring a smile to your face even when you aren't feeling yourself. They distract you and make you laugh when you don't think it's possible. Chris was a good dad. He always provided for his family like the man of the house is supposed to do. I kept thinking his reward will come someday. *The stress and hard work will pay off eventually. Just keep praying.*

Chapter 3

"January 2011"

The last week of January our oldest daughter had her first dance competition in Davenport, Iowa. We took the whole crew, plus my good friend, Erica, to help watch the little ones while our daughter was performing on stage. It was exciting to see the talent our daughter had at such a young age. Kristin danced to three songs. One song I remember so clear was "When Daddy Says I'm Beautiful." She wore this adorable baby pink costume, her hair in a performance bun, with stage make-up. She was beautiful and she loved the spotlight. The stage didn't frighten her – not once in her life. I clearly remember the second day she danced.

Chris was back and forth between the performance and the room that held the Chicago Bears play-off game on a large flat-screen television. I wasn't quite sure why he was so enthralled with this specific game. Nothing ever distracted him from Kristin's events.

That was an exhausting 3-day weekend of dance. The 4-hour drive home that Monday was a quiet one. I drove us all home which was very rare, but Chris had to get some work done so needed to be on his phone. He might have said five words the whole way home. Something was definitely off. *Maybe he's super stressed with work and doesn't want me to know.* Pride? Stress? I had three kids shouting from the backseat, so we were entertained all the way home. He told me on the way home that he had to do a site walk-through in Milwaukee and he needed to leave the next day. I thought, *okay, nothing out of the ordinary.*

Tuesday morning he left for Milwaukee, I went to work, kids went to daycare and school. I knew he would be home Wednesday so I could hold down the fort with our kids. No problem.

On Wednesday around 4:15 p.m., I began getting concerned. *He'd better get home soon, because I have to instruct a 5:00 p.m. fitness class.* He called and said he would be home in about 20 minutes. *Whew.* Not even ten minutes later I heard the door open. I said, "Who's here?" No one answered. *Chris? How bizarre! He's always accurate with time and he's early?* It worried me when he didn't respond when I asked who was here. He just silently walked inside and slipped around the corner. I was just thankful he was home in time so I could go teach my class. Twenty people would be waiting on me. I was running a Biggest Loser session at my gym, which required weekly weigh-ins, workouts and measurements. I got home from the gym around 6:30 p.m. and bedtime routine started. It was a busy night with three little kids, bath-time and brushing teeth. Chris and I often felt like two roommates raising three children. We passed each other throughout the house sometimes without even acknowledging one another. Our life was busy so this became our *normal*.

That night I was upstairs with our younger two kids and our oldest was downstairs. Chris and I hadn't slept in the same bedroom since our youngest was born. I was *that* mom that didn't like my kids upstairs without a parent being nearby. Plus, the intimacy in our marriage wasn't up to par anymore. There was some obvious distance between the two of us. Plus, our kids weren't feeling their best that evening. It was winter flu season at its peak. In the middle of the night I went downstairs to the kitchen to get some cold medicine for our toddler. I noticed the master bedroom TV was still on. *Hmmm...odd.* But I was so exhausted, I didn't bother going in to inquire. I just headed back upstairs. Sleep is very important when you are a mom of a five, three and 11 ½ month old!

The next morning we were all awake getting ready for work and school. Mornings were even more chaotic than evenings. Waking three sleeping kids, getting them fed and dressed and trying to make it to school and work on time is like managing a morning circus. As I stood in the kitchen with our three-year old son on my hip, I looked at him and whispered, "It's Daddy's birthday, let's tell him Happy Birthday." James and I said with excitement,

"Happy Birthday, Daddy!" Chris looked up quickly from the kitchen island to acknowledge what we said, and then looked right back down to the papers he was shuffling through. It's like he looked right through us. Or as if he heard a voice, got distracted, then went back to what he was doing. I just shrugged my shoulders and went on with the morning routine. I had picked up a few things for Chris's birthday the day before. As soon as he arrived home from work, I was all prepared to cook him a birthday dinner, have a birthday cake baked and ready and have the kids give him his presents.

James was ready for Daddy to take him to preschool. James went two half-days a week to his preschool. It was the same school I attended as a child, and my preschool teacher was still teaching. That was special to me. James grabbed his red preschool bag with his photo bag-tag hanging off the straps, I kissed James good-bye and off they went. Little did I know what was about to happen.

After my mom arrived to watch our five-year-old, Kristin, I took our youngest daughter, Norah, to daycare and went to work for half the day. Kristin wasn't feeling well so she stayed home that day with Grandma. I wanted to relieve my mom midday and be home early, so I only worked from 8:45–11:30 that morning, training a couple clients and calling it a day. Arriving home again, I walked in the house and started talking with my mom to see how everything had gone. Kristin seemed to be feeling better, but still had a low fever. Five minutes later there was a knock on the front door. I opened it to find the pastors from my church, Pastor Tom and Assistant

Pastor Dan, standing there with my Aunt Rebecca, staring at me like they just saw a ghost. *What's going on here? Does someone in the church need urgent prayer?*

Pastor Tom said, "Casey, it's Chris. He's been shot!"

Wait, what did I just hear? I said, "Oh, um is he okay? Where do I go to see him?"

Pastor says with hesitation, "He's at the Coroner's."

I'd heard the word *Coroner* once before, 25 years prior when my Great Grandma passed away. It didn't register with me until my mom grabbed my shoulders, my Aunt's eyes were full of fear, shock, tears...my daughter heard what Pastor said and screamed, "MY DADDY!" As my world came crashing down in just 30 seconds, I suddenly lost myself. I couldn't believe what I just heard. *It's his birthday. He has three beautiful children under the age of 5. We just built the beautiful home we were living in. I just saw him three hours ago and he took our three-year-old to preschool. What did I miss? How? Why? Where? Really?*

Then, the revelation came that he wasn't shot by some random act of crime or violence. He shot himself. *He killed himself.*

Within the hour family was pouring in. I remember sitting on my bed for hours that day, so confused and sad. I was devastated for my children. Many friends and family surrounded me. My church family was immediately dropping off food and other household staple items. I remember thinking, *so this is what happens when there is a death in the family?* Wait! It was my 35-year-old husband who died. *He's too young to leave me alone to raise these three kids by myself. What happened? Was I totally oblivious to something going on he didn't talk to me about?*

31

Was he depressed?

Everyone kept hugging me, crying and praying. *Why is this happening to me right now? How come I didn't pick up on what was bothering Chris? Was it something I did? Did someone do this to him?* My mind raced continuously. It wouldn't shut off. I couldn't sleep, I couldn't eat. When was I going to call his parents in Florida to give them the bad news? *How can I make that phone call?*

Then I started thinking of the past few days, few weeks, few months. We just had Thanksgiving and Christmas. He was a little more reserved at Christmas, but seemed fine at Thanksgiving. We had just taken our kids to Davenport, Iowa, for our daughter's first dance competition. She even danced to a lyrical song, "When Daddy Says I'm Beautiful." I wracked my brain. *Was there something I overlooked? How can he leave this world and these three beautiful children we created?* He was a good daddy! He was a good husband! He was well-liked in the community. He had a lot of friends. He was a good Christian man. He was involved with our church, attending every Sunday morning with our entire family. Chris went on quite a few mission trips with our church youth. *What was I blind to? Where did it all go wrong?*

The day was hectic. At one point I said with fear and anxiety, "What am I going to do?" My mom responded with, "Casey, look around you. We all love you and we will take care of you." I was in a frantic state of mind. People were still coming by, being very supportive. No time was a good time, but I knew it was time to call Chris's parents. I took my phone and sat in the only quiet room to give his parents the horrible news. The sound of their voices and shock was something disturbing I will never forget. A parent's worst nightmare come true. All I remember them saying after the initial bad news was, "We are going to pack up and start driving up tonight, see you soon."

I remember family just stood around the kitchen talking and asking about Chris and if he was any different these past couple weeks. We were all trying to put our heads together and think if there was something we missed. *How did it come to this?*

That evening I looked at my mom and asked her to take me to the site where Chris was found. My assistant pastor, Dan, was the last person to receive a text from Chris before he died. Chris had texted, "I can't do this anymore, please tell Casey and the kids I love them. I will be at the old farm house on the second set of curves off Route 29."

My mom didn't hesitate taking me because she, along with everyone else, wanted some answers. What was the significance of this property? We went looking late at night. I didn't care if we searched until sunrise, I wanted to know where he was found. All day my family was standing around talking and crying, I had to calm my curiosity.

We drove around country roads looking for the farm house. All we could follow were the red flashing beacon lights on nearby windmills, spanning miles and miles. There wasn't moon light or street lights to follow, so we focused on trying to find an outline of a house or building. Once my mom spotted the property, it took us another few minutes to find a road that lead to the site.

As we pulled up to the farm, we could see the tire tracks in the snow from his SUV. *This is the place.* We also saw the footprints of what I assumed were the police officers, coroner and whoever else was called to the scene. My eyes flooded with tears, my heart started aching, and before I knew it, I lost all control of my emotions again.

That feeling in my chest was so powerful. I was traumatized and I was hurting for my children. All that kept going through my mind was...*I just saw Chris this morning before work, James and I wished him a happy birthday, he dropped off our precious little boy at preschool right before he did this, and what was so bad that he felt the need to take his own life? What was he thinking while driving out here to this site? Was he crying before he pulled the trigger? Did he call anyone before he did this? Was he praying to God for help? Was he thinking of me and the kids? Was he running from something? Was he depressed?*

Chris's parents arrived the next day after driving all night. We hugged and cried for hours. I had no answers for them. We all just stared at each other with confusion. They had just been up to visit us a couple months prior for Thanksgiving, so it was just sad to think back on their last visit to Illinois with their son.

I had been in touch with the Coroner's office. The Coroner told me a note was found on Chris at the scene of the accident. My heart pounded at the news. She read it to me over the phone. I couldn't believe what I heard.

The farm property

Suicide Letter

To all those who love me I am very sorry for letting you down. At first I should have filed bankruptcy two years ago but I was afraid of what it would do to Casey's family. I did everything I could to not close those doors, as I could not face William and others if this happened. Looking back now I wish I would have done it. Now I am so deep I couldn't file without major consequences that would forever take me from my family. I love my wife and kids so much that I can no longer live with this pain. I don't sleep anymore and when I do, my dreams are so real it kills me inside. I hate Midwestern and ever being part of it. I should have walked away and let it go under long before I paid double what it was worth. Every time I thought I could get ahead I ended up hurting someone else. I have punished so many people, none which was done on purpose. I got myself to a point where I really believed I could turn things around. I let this business take everything from me that I love so much. This just shows people that you need to be happy with the simple life and love your kids with everything you have. I have no idea why God allowed me to purchase this company knowing it would fail and take me from my kids. My wife and business partners know nothing about what I have done in order to save this sinking ship. They continued to love me and support me. Every night I sit in my bed thinking of ways to end this all for good. On a good night when I really need sleep, I get myself to believe that it is possible to win the lottery and this all goes away. The truth is we can't change what is happening and it will continue to get worse. I am out of options and the pain is so strong it is killing me. I don't expect anyone to understand this but please trust me that I didn't want to hurt anymore. I did everything I could to save the company so I could watch my kids grow up to be great kids. I love my family and I hope someday you will understand how hard all of this was for me and that my decisions that I made were not made with bad intent.

I blame nobody but myself for moving forward on buying the business. I just wish that the sale of the business never got approved and my family and I still lived on 4th Street. I just don't understand as a Christian how God would let me buy this business, knowing it would fail and not be around to watch my kids grow up. My kids are everything to me and now I will not have them, and I can't live with that.

I am not a bad person and life has turned me into something I can't live with. My entire life I have always landed on my feet, but those days are over. My days were numbered the day I purchased the business. I don't know for sure and will never know, but God has decided that I was not going to be able to turn this business around. I can remember three months after buying the business that I paid way too much and that it would take a miracle to turn this around. The only miracle that I ever received was my three kids. I just hope someday they will learn and understand the truth of what happened.

The tears were rolling down my face again, my heart was physically aching in my chest as I read the suicide note once I held it in my hands. Never before had I experienced pain like that. At the bottom of the first page, a spot of his blood appeared, like a faded-red final signature, which broke me even more. My husband, once a loving father to three beautiful kids, vanished from this world and left me with this letter. *This stupid, precious, confusing letter.* I read the note over and over again, wondering why he seemed so angry about taking over the business from my dad. He repeated that over and over again. What does he mean by *"major consequences that would forever take me from my family"*? The suicide note didn't help, I was more sad reading the last thing he would ever write. The only thing he left for his children and I was a 2 ½ page written suicide note. I sobbed for hours, days, weeks.

The next day, my Dad offered to pick up all the

belongings found in Chris's vehicle. I was scared to see what my Dad came home with. I was also worried for my Dad, because I wasn't sure what condition Chris's SUV was left in. Was my Dad prepared to see repulsions the vehicle may contain? I felt like I was living in a horror movie and I was going to wake up soon from the nightmare. The Coroner kept the shotgun for the investigation, but everything else was emptied out of the SUV. I didn't care if I ever saw that shotgun again in my life. I'd seen it maybe once after Chris bought it from an auction.

When my Dad came back with the other items, we slowly went through each receipt and piece of paper found in his SUV. Nothing was making sense. *Why is there a receipt from a local airport in Central Indiana when he was in Milwaukee? Why was there a receipt from a gas station off the route home from Milwaukee?* Nothing at all was making sense. *He told me he drove on this trip, so why was he at an airport?* Was this the significance of the farm house where he was found?

We started going through his wallet to see if there was anything inside to give us answers. I called the company credit card 1-800 number to see where his last transactions were made. Chicago, Chicago, Chicago, Chicago...? *Why Chicago? He told me he went to Milwaukee.* Then I went to the Internet and looked up one of the names where the charge came from: "New Jersey Strip." *Maybe it's an expensive steakhouse?* My brother-in-law says to me, "Zoom in on that! That isn't a steakhouse, that's a strip club." *$650 dollars at a strip club? What?!? Why were their* *four different hotel charges for the same night?* Three charges were at a hotel by the airport, and one charge at a 5-star hotel downtown Chicago. *Why is there also a receipt for a restaurant at a local airport 30 minutes from our house? Who was he dropping off? Why wasn't he in Milwaukee like he said he was? What was he hiding from me? Who was he with?*

I immediately got angry. *Chris lied to me! He wasn't the man he said he was.* Enraged, I went into the master closet and pulled out all of his clothes and threw them on the kitchen floor. I didn't want to look at them again. I didn't want reminders of him. I told my cousin that she could give them all away. She decided to sell some things online. He had a nice wardrobe so she didn't want to just donate everything. You could say I went into an angry, raging temper for about 15 minutes. I continued my tirade and went into the mudroom. The kids' BB guns were on the top shelf. I took them down and threw them out on the garage floor. No guns, toys or real, would be in my sight ever again! I was lied to! I was deceived and so were my kids! How could I look at anything that he touched? As the rage subsided, I realized I needed to clear my head and focus on the positives in my life: my children.

We were living in a beautiful, custom built home on the golf course. We had only lived there for a little over a year. That home was our dream home, but I knew it was only a matter of time before the kids and I had to move because I wouldn't be able to afford living there on my income alone. I was okay with leaving it though, because the memories there would forever take me back to the horrible memories of that week.

Chapter 4

Planning the Funeral

While this was all going on, I still had to be a mom. Three precious children needed me to be there for them, yet I was dealing with planning a funeral. I had zero experience planning a funeral. My stomach was in knots. I had to choose a casket? *Why is that important, HE'S GONE! He's never coming back.* I had to write an obituary? How can I do that when all I can think of is – he's gone, he just left me, he just left his kids, how can I write anything positive about this man for his obituary? Panic set in about making funeral home decisions, adding to the overwhelm already covering me like a heavy sweater. *How do I plan a funeral service? I don't even know who's taking care of my children right now. Have they bathed, eaten, brushed their teeth? How much time should my kids stay home from school? If they return to school too soon, will other children bother my kids with hurtful questions?* I had a one-year-old baby, three-year-old and five-year-old who depended on me. They had to be so confused why so many people were in our house and why mommy was always crying.

The next day, the funeral director asked me if I wanted to view my husband the day before the visitation and funeral. *Yes,* I did. Because I still had a hard time believing he would do this to himself. Sadly, I had already planned our youngest daughter's first birthday party for the same day I'd need to view his body. The cake was made, family was already there at my house, and my parents thought it would be a good idea to just go ahead and have it.

Norah at her 1st birthday party, just three days after her daddy died.

Sunday morning came and I was preparing for the birthday party. My entire family decided we would stay home and listen to the church sermon on the radio because the thought of attending church was overwhelming. *Everything* at that point was overwhelming. I showered and tried to look presentable for my daughter's party. While standing in my master bathroom looking in the mirror, I noticed a couple people walking by my bathroom window. *Odd...*I continued getting ready and noticed more and more people. They kept coming! Then I realized these were all people from my church. *What are they doing out there?*

They kept walking around my house. Then they suddenly stopped, held hands and bowed their heads. They were praying! Their love and support flooded over me immediately. I couldn't believe they all came to my house on this cold winter day, stood there in heavy coats, hats and gloves and prayed over my home and family. The tears streamed from my eyes. This was one of the most memorable moments of my life. The love and support from our small town community was incredible. I had never witnessed anything like that before.

The birthday party came and went, and it was time to head over to the funeral home. My parents and Chris's parents went along with me for support. The five of us walked inside the front door and saw his casket set up at the front of the ceremony room. *There it is, oh God...* One portion of the casket was open for the viewing. It was the most foreign thing I have ever experienced in my life. For the last few days, my thoughts frequently wondered how he appeared at the scene of the accident. *Was he recognizable? What was I about to see?* My heart pounded out of my chest, hands and knees trembling. As I moved towards the partially-open casket, the thought hit – *I'm a 32-year-old widow viewing my husband after his suicide.* My parents let me walk up to Chris by myself, shaking with each step, still wondering when I was going to wake up from this nightmare.

The room was dim, only the light from a couple lamps in the far corners. Not only was it dim, it was also quiet; so quiet you could have heard a pin drop. As I approached the casket I saw part of his forehead and hair line. Only a quarter of his face was showing – the other three quarters covered by a Chicago Bears jersey. The funeral director told me she tried her best, "so your last look at him won't be so shocking and tragic." He was always clean shaven with a nice haircut, but I remember that winter in particular he let his hair grow longer and he had more facial hair than normal. He was a very handsome man. A tall, dark haired, blue-eyed, good-looking man.

So I stopped about a foot away from the casket, in shock, in disbelief about what lay there before me. My husband...my husband who I said "Happy Birthday!" to three mornings ago, was laying there dead, partially covered to hide the gruesome reality of his death. *He just took our son to pre-school. He just went with us to see our daughter's first dance competition. He just got home the other night from his work trip to watch the kiddos. Now he's laying here and I have no real answers.* I couldn't ask him what happened. I couldn't ask him why he left me and the kids. *Ten more minutes. Just ten more minutes with him is all I'd ask for.* With ten minutes, I wanted to ask him why he lied to me, why he was so hopeless. I was both sad for him and furious with him, but also so confused. He left me behind to deal with the lies and the mess he created for me and my family.

Those were his hands, his wedding band was on his ring finger. That was really him, this was for real. *He really is gone.* I reached in the casket and touched his chest. I had to see one last time if this was really him and yes, it was. For some reason I wanted it all to be a mistake; just a misunderstanding soon to be reconciled.

Then my parents joined me, respectfully, quietly coming to my side. It was a surreal moment etched in my mind. *I married this man six and a half years ago. We were going to grow old together and see our grandchildren grow up. Now what are my kids supposed to do without their dad who they love so much? What do I tell them now? What will I tell them in the future?*

Visitation and Funeral Service

The very next day was Chris's visitation and funeral. We planned for the services to be held at my church. It was time for me to see the public – time for me to witness everyone's shocking reaction to this horrible small-town tragedy. *What will I say to people coming through the line? What rumors and judgmental thoughts are swirling? How are my kids going to get through this funeral? How are they going to be affected after seeing a casket knowing their father is in it but they can't see him?*

44

Funeral home where I viewed him for the first time

The kids never viewed their daddy after he died. We made that decision so they could hold onto the fond, life-filled memories they have with him instead of having the memory of death.

As the service started, I remember feeling like a hollow shell as I stood in the front row. I felt weak and foolish. To this day I only remember three people, out of hundreds who attended and only one song that was played on the piano by a family friend, "Your Grace Is Enough." To this day, when that song comes across the radio in the car, James always says, "Hey mom, this is the song."

We decided not to do an open casket because of the gunshot wound to his face. I still found it difficult to believe I was never going to see him again. My kids were never going to have Daddy back. Just me; *the kids will only have me*. Chris will never see them celebrate another thing in their lives. He won't see them graduate high school or college. No braces or first kisses. He won't be there to walk them down the aisle at their weddings or see them become parents for the first time. My heart was hurting every hour of the day, and that day it ached even worse. *The kids must be so confused as to why their daddy is laying there in a casket at the front of the church. What will I tell them in the months and years ahead? Will I be enough for them? Will I have the right words to explain all of this in the future?* In the back of my mind, I knew God would give me the wisdom I needed when the time comes to share more with them.

At the front of the church was his closed casket, a large 16x24 photo of Chris on an easel, and a variety of plants and flower arrangements consuming the stairs and stage. *Stupid, beautiful flowers. I don't want you, I just want Chris back.* People filtered in and waited in line to give their condolences. My parents stood with me, and my kids were so young that they were sitting somewhere else with family. After a few hours of standing and people walking through the line, the service started. Like I mentioned, I only remember three people who I hugged out of the hundreds. The service was over and we drove to the burial site at a nearby cemetery. The discussion became all about the weather and how bad it was going to get later that day. It was an extremely cold winter day and a blizzard was forecasted. The graveside service quickly ended, just as the wind picked up and the snow started coming down. Bad weather was on its way. *Fitting, I suppose.*

All our family and friends went back to the church for the funeral dinner. People were leaving early because of the weather. It was absolutely the worst week of my life. I cried out to God, "Why, why God?" over and over again. *My husband is gone and I have no idea why, I just planned his funeral, I'm sitting at the funeral dinner still not able to consume anything substantial with my stomach in knots, and the worst winter storm just arrived.*

The trying, sad, exhausting day was coming to an end, thankfully. I just wanted to be home with my family and my children. That evening, my house was filled with every flower arrangement and potted plant from the funeral service. They filled my living room, kitchen and dining room, carrying dozens of different fragrances with them. Despite the thoughtfulness of everyone who gifted us flowers, I didn't want the constant reminders everywhere I turned, so I asked my family to please take any arrangement of their choice.

Chapter 5

Aftermath - The New Normal

What now? Where do I go from here? I had to adjust to the new normal. The normal for a few weeks consisted of my parents staying at my house. My sister, brother-in-law and their kids also stayed with us for a while. The trauma we all experienced was too much to handle alone. We were a close family to begin with, but this tragedy made us inseparable.

My business partner of Midwestern Repair, Zach, came by my house that week to give me some news and to deliver something he found on Chris's laptop. Zach said that Chris had a life insurance policy of one million dollars that is going to pay out. I didn't know he had a life insurance policy for such a large amount, and I was shocked a policy would pay out after a suicide. Zach was the first to give me some good news, that it was all going to be okay. He also said he'd found a different suicide note; a note left by Chris on his work laptop. The note sounded somewhat similar to the handwritten note found on Chris at the scene of the incident. The laptop note read exactly like this:

To whom it may concern:

I Chris owner of Midwestern Repair and Maintenance Service had made bad business decisions without other business partners being aware of these decisions. I did everything I could to save the company and keep it from going under and having people lose lots of money. I made these decisions with the intensions of fixing a problem that I purchased in '07 from William. William's accountant and my accountant were the same person and because of this I ended up paying double for a company that was in serious trouble before the sale. I was told by the bank that they would loan me the money to buy the company as they felt it was in the best interest of the company to have me own the company to try and turn things around. Shortly after buying the business, I decided we needed to grow the company in order to handle all the new bank payments we had with the sale of the business. The bank did not agree and could not loan me the money to help grow the company and I had to do it with the money we had coming in from the jobs we were doing. This hurt our cash flow every month and continued to put us behind. This continued to happen for years and it has finally reached the boiling point and is not salvageable. I have tried everything legal and not legal to try and save this company because banks don't lend to companies unless they have collateral for every dollar and we needed to grow and operate at a higher level. I even had a business partner come in and put a large amount of money into the company to help save the company and even that was not enough to turn things around because companies are taking 60-90 days or longer to pay. The State of Tennessee and Jasper County really hurt the company in '09 and '10 with slow pay or non-payment. The company was never able to turn things around after that.

I failed and I am responsible for the destruction of this company and I cannot live with the decisions I have made. I also cannot live with the fact that I have destroyed the Littleton and Nash families by bringing them into this company and failing them. If I could go back to last December I'd just file bankruptcy and save Zach and Betsy from all this horrible mess. I just hope they will be able to recover from this and not blame Casey and the kids for my disaster. Casey has always known that I am stressed about the company but had no idea what I have done to try and save the company and how bad it really is.

To my family:

I am truly sorry that I have failed you and that I am no longer around to be a husband and a dad. I cannot live with myself any longer and I cannot go to jail for my decisions as I would not survive one day. I just hope that you and the kids will be able to move forward without me and you will be better off. I know that our kids will be great kids and have lots of people who love them. I know they will probably never forgive me for being a failure and leaving them at such a young age. I have been driving around for weeks with a shotgun in my car and every day I wake up just wondering if today is the day that I will end my life. This is a horrible feeling and is a horrible situation. I do not ever want to disappoint people and that is what got me into this situation to begin with. I should have never purchased this company as I knew it was bigger than me and that I could not save it. I wish I would have walked away years ago and went and got a regular job and lived the simple life so I could enjoy my family and spend all my time with my kids. I love those kids more than anything and it destroys me to think about how bad they will think of me after this. I just hope someday that they will understand that I never wanted this and

I tried everything to get out of this situation so I could watch my kids grow up. I am so sorry, Casey, that I could not save this for us and that I failed you as a husband and provider. I am sure your dad will start his own company and make a go of it but I just hope he takes care of you and the kids as this was my fault and not yours. I am truly sorry and I love you very much and I know you will hate me for the rest of your life, but please believe me that I tried so hard to save this company.
Chris

It was heart breaking to read this second letter. Why he wrote a suicide note and then had another one on his computer was a mystery. I was just thankful Zach found it and gave it to me.

The first thing we had to deal with was the business. Along with family and friends, our employees were also left in shock. The president of the company was gone, so something major needed to be done. The employees were without work for a few days until we could sort through some things.

Zach decided to call a company meeting in order to get some things sorted out. The president of two different banks, my accountant and our attorney were there, as well as my parents and a couple other key employees. During that meeting we discovered the trouble the company was in. I thought, *so this is why Chris took his life?* All I knew at this point was he lied to me about where he went two nights before he died. *If only he'd known that if he communicated to us about the finances, we could all work together on a plan to come out from underneath. It didn't have to be this way.* Where all the debt came from still wasn't making sense. The company had work and employees stayed busy. Business was good, so we thought.

The weeks were filled with total chaos, spending hours and hours trying to find out what was going on and how and when the business made a turn for the worse. The topic of discussion at my house, every night, was this disaster we were all living through. Zach tried convincing me to invest the whole million dollar insurance policy back into Midwestern Repair because it was the only idea at the time to save the company. My dad wasn't fond of that plan. My dad said the company had been at low points before and we could certainly find a different way to dig ourselves out of the hole again. We held off on making any decisions for a few weeks. We are a family of great faith, so being prayerful before making major decisions was what we knew to do. We didn't just pray about it once or twice. We waited over a month to see what transpired.

My Dad and I went to lunch one afternoon the following month, and I remember dropping him off at his Midwestern office before I headed home. He had been going to the office off and on to see if any work needed to be done. He owned and operated the company for so long that he knew everything about the company and line of work. He was willing to do whatever was necessary to get the company out of the position it was left in.

I pulled into my driveway and saw my dad's truck speeding down the subdivision's road. I parked and got out as he walked up the driveway, saying, "I'm locked out!" I don't understand. He added, "My key no longer works for my office door."

I said, "How can that be, we were only gone for lunch?"

He said, "Zach had the locks changed while we were at lunch."

This wasn't making sense. This had been my dad's company for 30 years and we purchased the company from him just a few years ago. Why would Zach lock him out? My dad was the only employee with any knowledge of the business. We went inside and called our attorney. Once again, we sat confused, wondering why this took place. *My husband just died two months ago and now we are being locked out of our family business.*

A few minutes later we heard the doorbell. I opened the door to find an officer standing there, asking for me. He handed me official documents. Across the top it read: SUMMONS to Court. *I was just served papers for WHAT? A lawsuit for three million dollars? What in the world is going on? Why am I being sued by my best friend and her husband? My good friends and co-owners of the business just sued me? I've known them my whole life…why would they do this to me?*

Then it started to click. They were so angry about what my husband did, they wanted to come after me now. They want to blame someone, so they decided to turn their back on me. *This has to be why they locked Dad out of his office.*

The company was in huge financial trouble and it looked nearly impossible to dig a way out. Zach and Betsy decided to turn against me instead of work together to climb out of the financial debt my former husband put us all in. *Unbelievable!* The only thing I understood, along with them, was anger. I was angry too. Left alone with three small children to figure out life alone...angry. I was married to someone that wasn't being truthful to me...angry. He was obviously up to something and I was so foolish to not see the man I was married to...*angry.*

After hours of pondering why my dad would be locked out of his own business, our cell phones then had NO SERVICE. *No Service? What now?* My mom, my dad and myself were all on the company cell phone plan and had been for years. When we all discovered our simultaneous NO SERVICE problem, we were confused and hurt once again. We made a phone call to the company secretary only to learn that Zach also discontinued our health insurance. So in one day's time, he changed the locks on my dad's office door, our cell phones stopped working and we no longer had health insurance. Again, the feelings of betrayal exploded all around me – the first wound created by my deceased husband, and now another from my *good* friends and business partners.

This whirlwind of behind-our-backs drama wasn't settling well with any of us, but we knew it was wise to not react. We had to let our attorneys walk us through, step by step. My parents, sister and her family would meet at my house almost every night. Tragedy tends to pull family closer together. Despite the hurt, we depended on our faith to guide us through in order to survive the mess. After analyzing everything discovered after Chris died, we were suspicious of Zach's actions.

When people are guilty, they tend to be defensive and sometimes act out of impulse or anger. My sister was the first one to question whether the second suicide note was even written by Chris. Could it have been fabricated by someone else to cover up some suspicious acts? It was an interesting thought. *Why else would he lock us out of the company?* Zach told me he found it in Chris's drafts when he was going through the laptop, so I had no reason to question him at that point.

That very next week, Zach sent out a letter to all customers on Midwestern Repair and Maintenance Service letterhead announcing the tragedy that occurred and also announced his "transition to president is now complete." *Who made him president of the company? When someone changes rolls in a company, shouldn't a board meeting take place or some legal documentation?* We were appalled! Something wasn't adding up.

Throughout the Year: Summer 2011 – Spring 2012

Over the course of the year, after witnessing deposition after deposition and meetings with attorneys, we learned a forensic audit would be done on all of the company computers. If anything suspicious was going on, we would soon find out.

The forensic audit report showed there was, in fact, editing done on that suicide letter document after the date of Chris's death. After a thorough review of both suicide notes, the handwritten note found on Chris, was written the way Chris speaks and it was his handwriting. The suicide letter found on the laptop started with two paragraphs speaking of specific jobs, terms or specific years, and it didn't seem like it was written from someone getting ready to take their own life. It became obvious this wasn't written by my husband! The third paragraph sounds more like something Chris would have said and sounded very similar to the hand-written note. I was absolutely disgusted at the thought of someone adding information to a suicide letter in order to protect themselves. *Who in their right mind would do something like that? What was the big secret? Did someone in the company know something and didn't want anyone to find out? Why else would we be locked out of our own company?* Nothing felt right about this situation, whatsoever.

Anonymous Letter

My Dad received an anonymous letter that year. The letter was written from someone who seemed to know our family very well. This person knew of a meeting Chris had with the president of one of our competitors. The meeting even took place before Chris and I purchased the business in 2007. Interestingly, we found out Chris called the meeting to see if the competitor would be interested in buying the business after Chris took ownership. Why would Chris inquire about selling a company he didn't even own yet? Maybe he was trying to make a quick dollar. *Who would care enough about us to write this anonymous letter to my dad?* To this day we don't know who wrote it, but we are very thankful for the letter. Things like this surfaced on a monthly basis. We never knew what we'd encounter the next day.

Another Lawsuit

My goal that year was to keep the kids in their normal daily routines. They had school and daycare and I had a four-day work schedule. I was managing life between the legal storm I was in and being a single mother. It was normal for people in my community to come by my house unannounced or stop by my gym to check on the kids and I. Hearing my doorbell or a knock on the door was the new, welcomed normal. I may not have always had much to say when kind visitors showed up, but I did appreciate them. One weekday evening, however, I answered the door to find a Vanderburgh County officer standing there again! He handed over a new set of papers. *ANOTHER lawsuit?* This time it was demanding over $1.4 million and came from a bank Midwestern did business with. You are never mentally prepared for something like this, but at least I knew how to read the documents this time considering just a few weeks earlier my first court summons arrived. I was less blindsided now, only because I had a better under-standing how far my husband was in over his head, or else I wouldn't be getting lawsuits delivered to my front door. My attorney just added this to the list of items on my bankruptcy.

I was buried in paperwork, but continued to seek help from the only One above who could give me the strength to weather the increasing storm. Depending on the Lord to take care of us was the only thing I felt confident in. I also appreciated the supportive, loving, patient parents that I was blessed with. Words of wisdom from my mother over the years "God will not do what we can do,

He only does what we cannot do".

It was only a matter of time before the kids and I had to move out of the home we just built the year prior. I was thankful for the eight months we had in the house following Chris's death. I'm not sure I could have handled moving out right after the funeral. Our home sold quickly to a family I knew very well. I was at peace with leaving the home in their hands so we could walk away from the lingering memories those walls echoed. Moving was easier knowing someone would be taking good care of the home like I would.

The kids and I moved across town in October, 2011. A small rental home was available for $400 a month. The home was over 70 years old and it sat on a corner lot with a detached garage. I loved the area, because my childhood home was one block down the street. This neighborhood was filled with great memories for me. The rental house was a small, 2-bedroom home, but we made it work. Two of the kids shared one bedroom and my youngest had the other. The dining room was a good size, so I got creative and made it my bedroom, hanging curtains in the doorways.

I viewed life so differently after Chris died. We didn't need the boat, the nice car, the fancy golf course home, vacations, golf course memberships and brand new *everything* to make us happy. None of it mattered anymore. All that mattered to me was my kids' health and well-being.

Moving to that rental house was the best thing for us. We learned how to live simple and enjoy the small things in life. The kids were happy and that was all that mattered.

Halloween 2012 in the rental house

The months consisted of meetings with bankruptcy attorneys, my accountant and a different attorney for the estate. Outwardly I appeared to be holding it together, but the mess I was left in was more than I could fathom. The business debt Chris had me in was an amount I could *never* repay. I was a single mom working part-time at my gym to allow me the flexibility to be available more for my children. There were days I would wake up and convince myself to do something for the kids, even if it was something simple like swinging on our backyard swing set or taking them out for ice cream. My mind was full of doubt and insecurities, so mustering up motivation was nearly impossible. I felt foolish and extremely violated. My marriage was a joke. I didn't know which way to turn or who was trustworthy, so I learned to get comfortable living in my bubble, so-to-speak. My comfort zone consisted of a handful of people. If I was having a conversation with someone, I looked right through them, not giving them any credit. Deep down I believed everyone had ulterior motives. For a long time, I couldn't see the good in people. You could say I developed serious trust issues.

Growing up, my family was financially stable. At first we started out living paycheck to paycheck, but my mom did an amazing job taking care of us and our home, saving money, while my dad built a business with every ounce of energy he had. His efforts paid off, as he ended up being one of the most successful men in the industry. His hard work and dedication was known all over the country, even beyond our borders. He taught me if you put work into anything, do it right the first time even if takes a little more time.

I couldn't believe the position I was left in: bankruptcy, litigation being a single mom, etc. My previously perfect credit score meant nothing now. My name was thrown under the bus repeatedly. Everything I'd worked hard at for 33 years was questioned. Going back to college to do anything else wasn't feasible considering my three young children who needed my full attention. My head was spinning

As the year went on, my dad and I spent a lot of time driving back and forth to meetings or the courthouse. My dad was without a job, and we started to worry if my parents were going to be in financial trouble as well. Everything was difficult that year.

My attorney ordered depositions for most employees of the company – at least the ones who worked closely with Chris. I sat through at least seven depositions. When it came time to interview one of his female employees, I knew this deposition would be the one to gain the most information from. We all heard rumors, but the rumors that came back to me would be devastating if found to be true.

Serina's deposition went on for over two hours. It was nearing the end and my attorney and I stepped out in the hallway to see if anything else needed to be asked.

I said, "Yes, ask her if they had an affair."

My attorney said, "Do you really think she will confess?"

I said, "Just ask her."

We stepped back in the conference room and sat down. I was so nervous to hear this answer, because I didn't want the rumors to be true. I wanted to believe my husband left this world because of a situation he couldn't face *financially*. Pride can be a very dangerous quality, and deep down I wanted to believe that he wasn't capable of anything more. Following another question, my attorney then asked her, "Did you have any sexual relations with Chris?"

She replied, "Yes."

Once again my heart felt stabbed to the core, causing my whole body to shake uncontrollably. I immediately thought, *along with everything else he did financially, he was cheating on me.* Then my attorney asked her to elaborate. "Was this a one-time occurrence?"

She said, "It happened spontaneously."

My attorney asked her, "For how long was this going on?"

She said, "Throughout the last two years until right before he died."

I couldn't stop thinking of how that relationship developed, and *when did he have the time to be with her?* We were incredibly busy raising three kids and working every day. *When do people find the time to cheat? How could he be that type of father? How could he come home day after day and spend quality time with all of us and be living a second life with her? How could he look us in the eye or even be in the same room with the kids and I after being intimate with another woman? Horrifying.*

The deposition wrapped up shortly after that. Serina approached me afterwards and she was trembling, tears flooded her eyes. She said, "I'm so sorry, Casey." I said, "Thank you for telling me the truth, because I have not heard the truth in years, obviously." All I could think about was the lies. *So many lies. He was sleeping with her for two years. TWO years.* My son was only a year old at the time. I was nauseated. Thinking back, my kids and I would stop by to see Daddy at work during the week and his assistant would give my kids candy. We would sit in her office and chat with her about life. *How could she look me in the eyes all that time? People really do exist that live so unashamedly immoral? Do they have a heart at all? Do they care about the family at home?* I was never capable of cheating. I was a faithful wife. The day I said, "I do," my sexuality was settled. I knew that man would be the only man I would be with forever.

I was glad to be in the car heading home that day, but my mind wouldn't shut off. All I kept thinking was, *what else don't I know?*

Before 2011, I had never entered a courtroom. Unfortunately courtrooms became my home away from home, fighting the never-ending battle. My attorneys told me from the beginning, this would be a long process, and they were right.

If I could erase that year totally, I would. After enduring it, I realized I'd never fully be over what happened. Even so, I decided it was time to move on and focus on getting stronger. My children needed me. My sanity was torn in five different directions for over a year. Sadly, I felt like my kids were getting leftovers; leftovers of *me*. They would get the energy I had left after the day was over, which was very little. Was I the best mom at the time? Maybe not, but I was forced to be mom *and* dad, always there for them and determined to never fail them.

As the weeks and months went on, my kids had all kinds of questions. My five-year-old understood Daddy went to heaven and he wasn't coming back to live with us. I started seeing drawings like this around the house. Daddy and angels. Daddy sitting on a cloud. Daddy talking to Jesus. My daughter was such a smart, mature little five-year-old.

Drawing from Kristin

Single Parenting

This was the beginning of single parenting. I no longer had a husband to talk to throughout the day. I no longer could share the precious daily happenings regarding our children, or my day at work, or his day at work. How did God think I was capable of taking care of a home, paying the bills, taking care of our children and making all the decisions on my own from this point forward?

Thank God for my church family. They were truly amazing during that time. Some families brought meals over to us periodically. One couple would invite the kids and I over to their home for dinner and offered to help babysit if I ever needed someone. Another couple from my church sent me a $100 dollar check in the mail every month for at least 18 months. I couldn't believe the astounding generosity from these people. They indeed took the Bible literally when it says to give proper recognition to the widows.

"Give proper recognition to those widows who are really in need." (1 Timothy 5:3)

Before Chris's death, I never gave a second thought about how families who survived tragedy continued on with their lives. I never knew how much people were willing to help out, or should offer to help. The fact that families could really struggle with their finances or jobs afterwards was never a thought. It didn't dawn on me about possible psychological problems children could face in their future. I was oblivious to the aftermath of a tragedy.

One evening in particular stands out to me. A couple from my church invited us over for dinner, and on the car ride there my oldest daughter said from the backseat, "Mommy, someone said Daddy shot himself. Why would he shoot himself?" As my heart broke into another million pieces, I glanced to the back seat of the car and I responded with, "Honey, I don't think Daddy was feeling very well. I think he was very, very sad". That seemed to appease my five-year-old, thankfully. My heart was just aching for them. *They should never have deal with any of this at their ages.* Having to answer questions and give explanations like this was something I never imagined myself needing to do.

Story of Job

There were many nights I thought, why me? I often hear people say. "Why do bad things happen to good people?" It's a valid question.

Human suffering is everywhere we turn. For example, the book of Job addresses this ancient and unfortunate problem. Job was a godly man who endured an enormous amount of pain and suffering while remaining faithful to God. Job owned 7000 sheep, 3000 camels, 500 teams of oxen, and 500 female donkeys. He also had many servants. He was considered the richest man in the east. Satan wanted to inflict hardship on Job in hopes that Job would curse the Lord. Satan presented this plan to the Lord, assuming hardship would turn Job's heart away from the Lord. The Lord said, "All right, you may test him. Do whatever you want with everything he possesses, but don't harm him physically." Job 1:12

One day when Job's sons and daughters were feasting at the oldest brother's house, a messenger arrived at Job's home with horrible news. All of his animals had been killed. While that messenger was still speaking, another messenger arrived telling Job all of his servants had been killed. The last messenger arrived telling him, "Your sons and daughters were feasting in their oldest brother's home. Suddenly, a powerful wind swept in from the wilderness and hit the house on all sides. The house collapsed, and all your children are dead. I am the only one who escaped to tell you" (Job 1:18-19). Only Job and his wife survived the colossal tragedy Satan inflicted upon him.

Even though Job suffered a tremendous loss, not once did he curse God. Because of this, the Lord blessed Job in the second half of his life even more than in the beginning. He now had 14,000 sheep, 6000 camels, 1000 teams of oxen, and 1000 female donkeys (Job 42:12). The Lord also gave Job seven more sons and three more daughters. The Bible says in all the land, no women were as lovely as the daughters of Job.

Job lived 140 years after that, living to see four generations of his children and grandchildren. Then he died, an old man who lived a long, full life (Job 42:16). Tragedy heaped upon tragedy, and then redemption. I definitely related to Job's pain and was desperate to see my redemption come to pass.

Chapter 6

Life As I Knew It

Looking Back

As is typical with those left behind from suicide, I couldn't help scouring my memories for evidence; evidence of *why*. *Did I miss warning signs?* I continued to look back on the years we dated and our years of marriage to find anything out of the ordinary. I also asked Chris's family and friends a lot of questions, even about his adolescent years. *What did I miss?* Were there any signs of depression? I found out Chris had a high school girlfriend who broke up with him, and he acted out by stabbing himself in the abdomen with a wooden-handled steak knife. During his hospital visit, they tested him for psychological issues. His high school best friend said he was diagnosed with a bipolar disorder; a disorder associated with episodes of mood swings ranging from depressive lows to manic highs. A good friend of Chris's said he was prescribed medication but decided not to take the prescription. I tried to gather as much information about Chris as possible, hoping to discover what the root problem was and how he got to the low point of suicide.

Learning these new tidbits made me think back to a couple instances that didn't quite add up. In the year 2008, I specifically remember it was late in the evening, around midnight. The power was out because of a bad storm, and Chris told me he was going to run downstairs and check the sump pump. That was something he did often when it rained so our finished basement wouldn't flood. I was lying in bed, drifting off, and heard him tumble down the carpeted, enclosed basement staircase. I jumped up and ran to the top of the stairs and saw him lying on his back, moaning in pain with the flashlight by his side. He told me to call an ambulance. After the EMT's came to check him out, they said he was fine. This story doesn't add up to me. He wasn't a clumsy type of guy. He was tall, athletic and very coordinated.

Another instance that comes to mind is when Chris told me over the phone that he had a 101.3 temperature so he wasn't going into work that day. When I got home and talked to him face to face, I asked him where the thermometer was so I could take our daughter's temperature. He looked at me puzzled. I asked him again and he stuttered over his words. I said to him, "You told me you had a 101.3 fever, so where is the thermometer?" He said, "Oh, well...I was thinking it had to be at least that high, because I feel sick." *Hmmm.* I remember getting so upset at the time because he lied to me. Big or small, a lie is a lie. Some people might think *it wasn't that big of deal*, but if someone can lie so easily about little, insignificant things, then what more are they lying about?

Although I noticed he emotionally distanced himself near the end, he never seemed depressed in the eight years I knew him. He always seemed upbeat and honest, so I obviously overlooked some things or he had an amazing game face. I usually hear of this kind of thing happening to other people, never imagining it would happen to me. He did make large, spontaneous purchases on occasion. We were the married couple who had separate bank accounts, so if he wanted to make a small or large purchase, usually it was fine with me. It didn't affect my checkbook. Now I realize those spontaneous purchases weren't what people would call *normal*.

One day, all excited, Chris called to inform me he planned to buy a red Hummer H2. "It's located in California though, so I will just fly out there and drive it back," he stated. What was I supposed to say to that? He obviously was going to sell his current vehicle, so I hoped all would be well. Another time he purchased a pop-up camper, but after a one-time use, he upgraded to a large, pull-behind camper. We only used the pop-up camper once and he was ready to be done with it. We also had a really nice Rinker boat, but that lasted one summer before he upgraded to a bigger boat. We ended up selling the boat the April before he died. We couldn't find the time to go boating with three small children. I was aware of his purchases but it didn't alarm me. I assumed he had the financing all figured out. Chris wasn't the type of person to ever plan in advance. If he wanted something, he made it happen on the spot.

It wasn't until 2010 that I recall another strange instance that seemed alarming. Chris was complaining about bad stomach pains. He had a family history of Crohn's Disease, which is a chronic inflammatory disease of the digestive track. The symptoms include abdominal pain and more. He said he was having so much pain that he needed to visit a Gastroenterologist so they could do a colonoscopy. I was at the hospital with him when the doctor came to his bedside with the results from the scope. The doctor said happily, "Chris, everything actually looks really good! Healthy!" The look on Chris's face was unforgettable. He continued to show signs of pain even though the doctor ruled out Crohn's. Looking back on this, it's almost as if Chris wanted something to be wrong with him. *Was he seeking attention? Was he acting out for something?*

A couple months before Chris died, I remember opening up all of our mail for utilities and credit cards one day. I typically placed the mail in a stack by the refrigerator for Chris to take to work, because he paid his bills at his desk. That one time I thought I'd help him pay bills to relieve some of his stress. I was an excellent money manager and followed a strict budget for myself. Since Chris was highly stressed all the time, I took it upon myself to formulate a plan for him to pay loans and cards down so he could relax some. While opening all the bills, there was one from the company that financed our boat. When Chris got home from work I remember asking him, with confusion in my voice, "We sold the boat in April right, so why are we still getting a payment statement in the mail?" He said, "Oh, that must be a mistake, I will handle it." Why would I question him any further? I trusted him.

Looking back, the new owner of the boat called Chris several times asking for the title on the boat, and Chris kept telling him, "It should arrive any day," and, "I will call and check on that." I specifically remember Chris ignoring his phone call once or twice. It turns out he never paid off the balance for the boat's loan. Where that boat sale money went remains a mystery.

I had a couple different conversations with James's preschool teacher, since she was one of the last people to see him alive. I asked her, "How did he seem when he came in the room to drop off James?" She said, "He just walked in with him, hugged him and said bye. He wasn't talkative at all." Little did James know that was the last hug he would ever get from his daddy.

Crying became a typical part of my day. I tried protecting my children from seeing how broken I was inside. My faith in God was still there, but I was weak and confused. There were many nights when I would just fall to my knees in tears. My knees gave out as I was overcome with emotion. Some days I would be driving in the car, minding my own business, and a certain song would come on and hit me like a slap in the face. I couldn't listen to it. Occasionally my route took me on the road that passed the site where Chris was found, and I would uncontrollably bawl my eyes out.

The summer before he died, a popular song was released called, "If I Die Young" by The Band Perry. The kids and I would be on the swing set with the radio playing and that song seemed to come on often. We loved it and would all chime in singing, loudly. I remember a time when Chris was sitting outside on the deck, talking on his cell phone while watching our kids on the swing set, and that song was playing. After the funeral, it took me six years to be able to listen to that song all the way through.

Being a Single Mom

Here's an interesting statistic from the U.S. Census Bureau (in Nov. 2016): the majority of America's 73.7 million children under age 18 live in families with two parents (69 percent). The second most common family arrangement is children living with a single mother, at 23 percent.

I couldn't shake the negative "single mom" stigma. I was that mom in the room without a husband. My kids were those kids in school without a dad. I was a statistic. At my kids' sporting events or school concerts I often thought, *their dad would sure be proud of them. He's missing out on so much. He should be here.* I always ask God in prayer, "Lord, did you really plan for me to do this alone?" You must think I can do this single-mom life, because You are giving me the daily strength to get through it." To this day I still sometimes ask, "God, why?"

Mornings and evenings were the most difficult. Waking up three children under the age of five and getting them dressed, fed breakfast, cleaning breakfast up, hair done, teeth brushed, lunches made, and off to school on time is comparable to a circus. In the evenings, homework had to get done, dinner cooked and cleaned up, laundry done, bath-time, teeth brushed, and bedtime. I was running laps around my house constantly, never getting a break. Their dad was never coming back to be there for his kids. While the circus routine became the normal, I still had to find time to meet with attorneys, work at my gym and get the children to their dance and baseball events. My head was spinning with schedules, phone calls and meetings, all while I was still confused as to why my husband left us in the first place. *There has to be more I still don't know.*

Grieving Support Group

A few months after Chris died someone recommended a group grieving class, so I gave it a try. Everyone in that class seemed sad. They lost a parent, a child or a spouse, but no one there experienced hot anger, lawsuits and litigation following their loved one's death. I couldn't relate well to anyone in there. None of these people had been married to a con-artist. The sadness I felt was for my kids. The anger I still carried was at Chris for leaving his mess for me deal with.

The group grieving class ended up not helping me. I felt more frustrated afterwards than I did when I arrived. Since I didn't have a connection with that group, I tried one-on-one counseling sessions. That was my first time in one-on-one counseling. Up till then, counseling had a stigma to me. *Only crazy, mentally unstable people needed to see a shrink!* Well, that couldn't have been farther from the truth. Counseling, therapy, shrink sessions, whatever you want to call them, are extremely helpful. Yes, that counselor is getting paid to hear you unload your anger and hurt, but it's healthy to unload. Talking to someone about what is bothering you is very therapeutic. I often wonder if Chris would have sought help, maybe he would still be here today.

Second Chance at Life – Trying to Get Out

I really tried moving on after the funeral. I'd never lived through something so traumatic and life-changing. Five months after the funeral my 33rd birthday was approaching and a few of my high school friends invited me to go boating with them. At first I thought, *I'm not in the mood to have fun and socialize. That requires talking and being dressed in something other than sweatpants and a t-shirt.* Then I thought twice. *Gosh, I need to quit moping around in my house for just a day and go with my friends to enjoy some sunshine on the lake.*

My sister planned to watch my kids for me, so I didn't have to worry about getting a babysitter. We all spent the night at my sister's house the night prior. As I left early in the morning, driving down her long, country, gravel lane, the song "Stronger" by Sara Evans came on the radio. The memory of that morning was like it happened yesterday. The first part of that song replayed in my mind for months. Sara sang about waking up with the pain, but getting dressed and putting a smile on anyway. Riding to work, trying to ignore her hurts and a song comes on. She's reminded of the person she misses, but realizes she's getting stronger, bit by bit.

As I listen and drive down a two-lane highway, tears once again pour down my cheeks. Since Chris died, I'd felt the pain stinging every single day. Getting out of bed each day was an accomplishment in itself. I was living a widowed, courtroom nightmare and I still had to get up and carry on to be the best mom I knew how to be. At that point in time, listening to the Christian music stations was hard. Everything reminded me of the funeral. I rarely could sing through an entire praise and worship song at church on Sunday mornings. I had to push the memories away of Chris's casket sitting at the front of the sanctuary at church. Tears were my daily friend and enemy. Yes, my kids did see me cry sometimes, but if I didn't camouflage some feelings, crying could have completely consumed me. I was not going to allow myself to go down a dark path. God continued to show me that He's got this. I had to let go and let God.

It took a lot of emotional and scheduling effort for me to plan something like this, so going on the lake with friends was a big deal and a major feat. We arrived at the lake's campground, unpacked our bags and walked down to the boat. My friend, Jana, introduced me to a couple guys who were waiting on the dock. I didn't care about meeting new people, especially guys.

The day started with a relaxing boat ride on Lake Wawasee. Two other boats plus ours, made a run down the lake. About one hour into the day we started to see dark clouds rolling in. Soon after that, it was a torrential downpour! That wasn't exactly how I saw the day starting out. Within an hour the sun was back out and everyone tied up in a cove to relax. I forced myself to enjoy the adult time and not worry about what others knew or didn't know about me, about whether or not the kids were okay, etc. making light conversation with a couple guys on the other boat, I asked them their names, not remembering I was introduced to them an hour prior. Obviously my mind wasn't 100% focused on small talk.

So I continued mingling and found I was actually relaxed enough to laugh again, no longer feeling like an outcast.

It was difficult for me to let my guard down with anyone and truly enjoy my days and nights. My mind was foggy every single moment, with the weight of the world on my shoulders. Having fun was the last thing on my mind, because it conflicted with the obvious struggle I couldn't escape from.

Nearly two years after Chris's suicide, I remarried a man I met at the lake that day. After four years together, two miscarriages and the precious birth of our daughter, my fourth child, we went our separate ways. We had our differences and decided we were better off divorcing. I'll share a little bit more about instances and events during those four years in the next several segments.

Full, true grieving was something I never let myself experience. Through the years I may have been smiling, but deep within my smile was a silent sadness. I knew my heart was not healed.

"Even in laughter the heart may ache, and joy may end in grief." (Proverbs 14:13)

Moving After Chris Died – August 2013

During my second marriage, I was faced with the decision to move out of my hometown. It was hard for me to think of uprooting my children to a new community, but it made the most sense. I had permanent scars now from my hometown and everywhere I turned was a memory of Chris.

We were renting a house in my hometown at the time we got married, and the owner decided it was time to sell. The listing price of the home far exceeded what we could afford, and there was nothing else available in our town to suit our family's needs. I had to consider moving away, possibly closer to Indianapolis, where my new husband drove to work five days a week. As difficult as it was for me, the only thing that made sense was to move to his hometown. *Why move to just any town when we could be closer to some of his family?*

I remember the day I made that decision. I shed a few tears before, during and after having that final conversation. Our minds were made up and we were moving 40 miles away.

Once the kids were registered for school and we were settled in our new house, my stomach was no longer in knots. Watching the kids blossom in a new school atmosphere was all I needed to see. They would come home from school with beaming smiles talking about their classes, new friends and what happened at recess and lunch. I'm so thankful for their kind, understanding teachers, Mrs. Whitson and Mrs. Hanson. The transition to a new school wouldn't have been as easy if it weren't for them. I never informed the school staff about what my children had gone through. They only knew my husband was their step-father, not their real dad. Discussing the tragedy was something I tried to suppress for as long as possible. Here in this new town, people didn't know. It was like a fresh start. But, if the timing was right during a parent teacher conference, then I would elaborate more so the teachers would have a better understanding.

Postpartum Depression

After my fourth child, Holly, was born, it was painfully obvious I was suffering from postpartum depression. With an unhealthy mind and marriage, a precious newborn baby and my three young children that just lost their dad a few years prior, I was gloomy most days.

What is postpartum depression? The birth of a baby can trigger a jumble of powerful emotions, from excitement and joy to fear and anxiety. But it can also result in something you might not expect: depression. Postpartum depression isn't a character flaw or a weakness. Sometimes it's simply a complication of giving birth.

Symptoms may include:
- Depressed mood or severe mood swings
- Excessive crying
- Difficulty bonding with your baby
- Withdrawing from family and friends
- Loss of appetite or eating much more than usual
- Inability to sleep or sleeping too much
- Overwhelming fatigue or loss of energy
- Reduced interest and pleasure in activities you used to enjoy
- Intense irritability and anger
- Fear that you're not a good mother
- Feelings of worthlessness, shame, guilt or inadequacy
- Diminished ability to think clearly, concentrate or make decisions

- Severe anxiety and panic attacks
- Thoughts of harming yourself or your baby
- Recurrent thoughts of death or suicide

(Postpartum depression information according to mayoclinic.org)

I was afraid to admit it, but as I read through mayoclinic.org, I had over half of the postpartum depression symptoms on the list. I even experienced my first panic attack at nine weeks pregnant, so I knew this pregnancy's hormone levels were like nothing before. When that panic attack hit, my five-year-old daughter and I were driving into town, and suddenly noticed it was hard to breathe. I was gasping for air and started to get light-headed. I rolled my windows down, picked up my cell phone and dialed my mom's number. By the time she answered, I had pulled the car over and could barely get any words out. "Ma...I can't...breathe," and right away she said, "Lean your seat back and try to take deep breaths." I was so scared. My daughter was in the car, not understanding what was happening, but I couldn't even respond to her. The feeling of helplessness is scary. Thankfully my mom talked me down and also talked to my daughter.

Even during pregnancy I recognized I was depressed and wasn't in the healthiest mindset. I still wasn't, so I visited my doctor and told him everything from the beginning of the pregnancy, to the postpartum feelings I was having.

I wasn't in a healthy frame of mind. I had to put my fears aside and let God take the reins. Scripture says,

"Come to me, all of you who are weary and carry heavy burdens and I will give you rest." (Matthew 11:28)

When Plexus Started

One fall afternoon, a friend of mine, Raegan, contacted me through Facebook. I hadn't talked to her in a long time. She was a busy mom of five kids and her top priorities were God, family and health, much like mine. She wasn't like any friend I've ever had. First of all, she was my only friend with more than three children, and second of all, she was my only friend that gardened and made most of her meals from scratch. I was very intrigued by how she did it all. Her wisdom of the Bible and her unconditional love for her family was something that made her stand out.

Raegan's Facebook message read, "Hey Casey, how have you been? I've been drinking this new pink drink for a while and it honestly helps with sugar cravings! I know you have a sweet tooth, so I just wanted to reach out to see if you wanted me to send you a sample!" Sounded interesting, but I was breastfeeding Holly at the time so I really didn't want to try anything new. Raegan reassured me the drink was 100% safe for pregnant and nursing moms. Plus, this information was coming from the Super Mom of all moms. I trusted her completely. She sent me a sample and it was delicious! From that point on I was hooked! I couldn't believe the magic potion was actually keeping me away from junk food. I had no idea that one pink drink sample was the beginning of a new journey in my personal development, my Plexus journey.

Plexus was so much more than good supplements. The amazing coaches and leadership available to me and the endless amounts of resources at my fingertips had a lot to do with where I am at today. The first book I ever read from cover to cover during this journey was called *Go Pro* by Eric Worre. *Go Pro* was recommended by another woman who reached the highest rank in the company. I was intrigued by how she earned her way to the top, so I was determined to try everything I could to learn the process.

Our baby was only eight months old and I was learning a whole new business. Starting something new was not what I saw coming, but everything about it felt right. Since my marriage was on the rocks, I decided to focus on what was helping me grow on the inside. My self-esteem was lower than it ever was before, but trainings and learning opportunities through Plexus offered me something valuable. Postpartum depression knocked on my emotional door every day, so I was grasping for hope.

As the year went on, I ranked up in the company, earned my way to a leaders retreat, and then ranked up again. I didn't see myself as a leader. Sure, I'd successfully led fitness classes and a household of kids, but I never viewed myself as a strong leader. During this time I read through books as fast as I would go through a box of cereal, which was fast for a mom with four kids. I was challenging myself even more than I did in college. New thoughts, ideas and a sense of personal empowerment encouraged me greatly. This business was helping fill the void I had in my life.

After Divorce

The divorce took almost a year to finalize. During that time I turned to counseling and a divorce care group at my church. Once again, I felt like I took several steps backwards in my journey. My husband died just six years earlier and I was still just treading water. Was I ever going to make it out of the storm? Was I ever going to have an easier go at life? A suicide, now divorce? *What am I doing wrong?*

This was a period of time I did a lot of self-reflecting. I was open to new friendships and dating but it wasn't my first priority. I started journaling more and reading the Bible again.

Crime Scene Photos

During this time I was still processing my divorce and still going through a lot internally. I never fully had closure from Chris dying so I felt mentally scattered most of the time. Being able to focus my attention on one thing effectively was difficult. I had often wondered how Chris was found the morning he shot himself. I knew it might be a long shot but decided to call the Monroe County Police Department and request the crime scene photos from 2011. Six years had passed and I felt I was in a good enough place to view something that graphic, if they even would release them to me. Sure enough, after going through the proper request, they mailed me the DVD that contained the images. I was dating someone briefly at that time and I ended up telling him I was going to view the crime scene photos as soon as I received them. He understood my curiosity, but wasn't sure I should be alone when seeing them for the first time. I agreed to wait until he was with me to open up the DVD.

That day came two days later. My anxiety was through the roof as we loaded the disc on the laptop. There were hundreds of images, so we started from the top. *What kind of photos do police officers take at scenes like this?* I wondered. I had no idea what to expect, but I patiently went through each one. After opening up about half of them, I knew we were approaching the photos taken inside Chris's Suburban. The photo of the farm house from a distance didn't get me rattled, because I have driven past that property many times since his death. However, the interior photo of his driver's door stirred up some tense emotions. It showed some remains from the impact of the shotgun. Part of his jaw and teeth were there, and spots of blood on the seats. He was not in the driver's seat though. Next we came to photos of the bucket seats in the middle row of the vehicle. I saw a pair of shoes our son had in the car and the kids' car seats. More blood was also visible there, but nothing too bad. At this point I started to shake, knowing what we were about to see.

In the previous photo I could see the tip of Chris's shoe on the floor of the third row seat of the SUV. *He went to the back. For six years I have wondered about so much, so many unanswered questions.* I was seconds away from seeing my husband, the father of my three precious children, in the saddest, most gruesome state possible. *Am I strong enough to handle this?*

The final photos were opened. The first thing I choked out as tears filled my eyes was, "Aww, Chris..." Then I broke down. He was sitting in the third row bench seat with the shotgun resting by his left thigh, hands still on the gun, head resting against the back window. His face was unrecognizable. I could see his hands, his wedding ring, his clothes, and I knew that was him, but not the man I once married.

Somewhere on Chris's journey he turned down a dark path. One bad decision led to the next bad decision and eventually he couldn't live with the heaping pile of guilt anymore. Strangely, seeing him in this horrible state did give me closure. Some might think they'd never want to view photos like that of a loved one, but I was actually glad to put one more piece of the puzzle together for my own sanity's sake.

During this time, my ex-husband and I were starting to share custody of our young daughter. The drop offs and pick-ups were emotional for me. It was difficult for me to see my broken family. So many different emotions surged through me. My past was affecting me and I knew it. Healing would take months or maybe years to complete with the proper counseling and a lot of prayer.

Joining a Small Group

I was searching for answers and for years I'd considered joining a small group at church, and I finally inquired about it. I wanted to find a group of moms like myself who met on a weekly basis to study the Bible together, but mostly, I wanted support from a group of other moms. I always assumed people who participated in Bible studies were extremely wise and knowledgeable about all the Bible stories and their lives were probably close to perfect. Ha, that was far from the truth!

A small group welcome meeting was held one Sunday evening at church. Approximately 40-50 people attended, splitting off into different sections of the church according to what type of small group they wanted to join. Group options were things like women's groups, men's groups, young married couples, empty nesters, and so forth. I chose to be a part of a women's study group. Next, they divided us up according to which nights worked with our schedules. About six ladies, including myself walked over to the Sunday evening group. We all stared at each other as if we were second-guessing our decision. *Should I do this?* Not one of us was super comfortable at first, but we all were there with the same intention, to learn more about the Bible with the support of a like-minded, small group of people.

I was hungry to know more about the Bible and I was stepping outside of my comfort zone to engage with others for support. Everyone needs an accountability partner, right? That is exactly how I looked at my small group: people who will help me grow. I was grasping for something that I couldn't put into words at the time. But looking back, I was ready to take my next step in healing. My small group was just the beginning of new spiritual growth.

During this season of life I had another obstacle I

couldn't seem to figure out. *Why am I dating someone who I don't 100% see myself having a future with?* I didn't connect with him spiritually or emotionally, so *what am I doing?* I was treading water for some unknown reason, looking for someone to lean on. My small group would become those *someones.* We continued to meet each week until that study was complete. By this time, winter was in full force.

Depressed in February

Flu season was at its peak in mid-February. All four kids were sick and then I ended up getting sick, too. Along with the illness, I was falling into a case of the winter blahs. During my slump of trying to get everyone healthy again, I pondered more about why I was dating a man I didn't see a future with. Was I suffering from seasonal depression? *Why am I in a slump?*

I found myself reaching out to my friends and I would call my mother often. I didn't want to be that "negative Nancy" person people try to avoid. That wasn't who I was. *What happened to the positive, sarcastic, fun-loving me?* Something needed to change, and quick.

Since I didn't see a future with the man I was dating, I quickly broke everything off. Even though I may not have confronted him about my concerns in the beginning of our relationship, *better late than never.* We shouldn't date someone expecting them to change for us. Sometimes we just need to realize two people aren't meant to be. I wasn't going to be trapped in another rocky marriage if I saw all the signs to walk away in the beginning. Maybe I was gaining wisdom from my past experiences. Just maybe I was starting to make better decisions.

My heart broke with the thought of telling the kids. They had grown attached to him in some ways, and I was sad for both of our families. The unfortunate part is the loss of another relationship, even though I knew it was the right decision.

My mind was no longer clouded by the weight of indecisiveness. I could now move forward with a clean slate and focus on the four precious gifts I had in front of me: my children.

Learning anything of great value takes time. I was determined to be the best mom I could possibly be. I started turning to God in prayer, often on my knees. Yes, for the first time in decades, I bowed down in prayer. I was giving it all to the Lord. *Please, Lord, take everything I am. I want to be in Your perfect will for my life.*

On my 40-minute drive to work, I would listen to In Touch Ministries with Dr. Charles Stanley. His sermons spoke to me like nothing else I had ever heard. Something was moving inside of me, changing, and I had never experienced that feeling before. God gave me a peace that I can't describe. I didn't earn it, nor did I deserve it.

Value of Marriage

With one divorce and one broken relationship behind me, the thought of disappointing my children kept weighing on me. Marriage is an enormous decision and a promise not only to each other, but also to God. It's certainly not just a dating game to play for a while, and if it doesn't work out…then bail. Good marriages consist of love, commitment, humility, patience, forgiveness, quality time, honesty, trust, communication, and selflessness all centered around God. It is a gift from God, and part of His plan for us. It's best to marry a person you respect, love, enjoy and feel comfortable with.

My goal is to teach my kids that marriage is a commitment involving daily effort. Sadly, you can make daily effort with the wrong person and suffer the consequences. Or instead, you can wait for the right person to be in your life; someone who adds value and who's a positive influence on you. We are all given a free will. Some of us choose to be influenced by the peer pressure of today's society. Others choose to seek out what God has in store for them. It can be a waiting game to truly find Mr. or Mrs. Right, and in today's world, patience is a virtue.

We live in a world of speed and efficiency. We want fast food, fast service and fast resolutions to every situation in life. Many of us get impatient and want someone to pay for not doing something when we want it to be done. The actual definition of patience is "the capacity to accept or tolerate delay, trouble or suffering without getting angry or upset."

One particular story in the Bible stands out to me regarding patience: the story of Abraham and Sarah. God promised Abraham that he would have descendants as numerous as the stars (Genesis 15:1-6). This was despite the fact that Abraham and his wife Sarah were childless, unable to have children when they were younger, and were (seemingly) much too old to have children at the time of this promise. However, we do know that Abraham believed God anyway, and God accounted it to him as righteousness despite their advanced age (Genesis 15:5-6). Even though God reinforced the promise over several years, when the promise was not fulfilled right away, Sarah suggested that Abraham take Sarah's handmaid Hagar to have a child (Genesis 16). Abraham took her advice, Hagar became pregnant and the resulting child was Ishmael. It was not until many years after the original promise when Abraham was 100 years old and Sarah was 99 years old that the true promise was fulfilled by the birth of Isaac through Sarah (Genesis 17:15; Genesis 21:1-8).

Because Isaac was the child of promise, not Ishmael, it caused great friction in the household. The inheritance of Abraham would go to Isaac, not Ishmael who was older. The repercussions of this hasty decision continues to this day through descendants of Ishmael (Arabs) and the descendants of Isaac (Jews) as they continue to fight over who should own the land in the area of Palestine.

Another story that stands out to me in the Bible was about Job. God considered Job to be a man who was perfect and upright in all his ways (Job1:1, 8; Job 2:3).

Satan discussed Job's "perfectness" with God, trying to imply Job's faith was simply a byproduct of God's protection. He supposed Job's faith would crumble once God's blessings and protection were gone. So, God allowed Satan to test Job by attacking Job's livelihood, his family and his physical body. Satan's attack was so vicious, even Job's wife told Job he should give up – just curse God and die. Her lack of support was just another line on the long list of Job's troubles, but despite this, Job rebuked his own wife and still refused to curse God (Job 2:9-10).

Job continued to search for answers as to why this was happening to him. It wasn't until Job examined himself and cried out to God that God answered Him and set Job straight. Job believed what God said, and God blessed Job abundantly above and beyond how He had blessed him in the past.

Each of these stories has a different view on patience. Abraham and Sarah had patience to a certain point, but they decided to take matters into their own hands. As a result of their actions, long-lasting family struggles were created. In Job's case, he was a man patient enough to ignore bad advice, wait on God and trust in His timing. He knew God would give him an answer to his trials eventually, and He did.

Those two Bible stories come to my mind often. I lost my husband to suicide and he literally left me to fight the trials *he* caused. At the time I remember sitting in the courtroom just wanting it all to go away, *right away*. I was overwhelmed and wanted things to be over on my terms. My future was in question, and I wanted God to immediately speak to me.

Looking back, I wasn't leaning on God for strength like I should have been. I leaned on my own (nearly non-existent) strength, causing me to be impatient and extremely frustrated, broken and emotional. After that tragedy, I hastily got remarried; a marriage that was very unhealthy. Because of the marriage issues, I was in prayer often, but not often enough and not about the deep issues of my heart. I read the Bible, but never once *studied* the Bible or joined a study group for support. Again, I wanted things done on *my* terms, *my* way. I knew a lot about God, but didn't have a personal relationship with Him. Sooner or later (I wish it had been sooner) it became apparent I wasn't going to get the answers I was desperate for by continuing to do life *my* way.

I learned so much during that time period in my life. For the first time ever, I learned to focus on healing, grieving and being a good mom. Being on the *patience bandwagon* wasn't so bad after all now. I was submitting to God's will and focusing on Him. When we focus on Him, the earthly things don't seem to bother us as much. It was time to dust off the Bible in my nightstand and allow the wisdom to change me from the inside out rather than give me momentary doses of comfort.

One day, I came across an old bookmark I'd received at a ministry conference a couple years before. The large bookmark had lists of Bible verses for when a person is struggling and doesn't know where to turn. This would have been an excellent list for me every single day. Literally and physically there were many times in my life when I didn't know where to turn. The verses that spoke to me the most are these:

When you are afraid or worried

Psalm 91 talks about God's protection in the midst of danger. God doesn't promise a world free from danger, but He does promise His help whenever we face danger.

Psalm 107:28 *"Then they cried out to the Lord in their trouble, and he brought them out of their distress."*

Proverbs 3:5-6 *"Trust in the Lord with all your heart and lean not on your own understanding; in all your ways submit to Him, and He will make your paths straight."*

Isaiah 41:10 *"So do not fear, for I am with you; do not be dismayed, for I am your God. I will strengthen you and help you; I will uphold you with my righteous right hand.*

Matthew 10:28-30 *"Do not be afraid of those who kill the body but cannot kill the soul. Rather, be afraid of the One who can destroy both soul and body in hell. Are not two sparrows sold for a penny? Yet not one of them will fall to the ground apart from the will of your Father. And even the very hairs of your head are all numbered."*

2 Corinthians 4:16-18 *"Therefore do not lose heart. Though outwardly we are wasting away, yet inwardly we are being renewed day by day. For our light and momentary troubles are achieving for us an eternal glory that far outweighs them all. So we fix our eyes not on what is seen, but on what is unseen. For what is seen is temporary, but what is unseen is eternal."*

2 Corinthians 12:10 *"That is why, for Christ's sake, I delight in weaknesses, in insults, in hardships, in persecutions, in difficulties. For when I am weak, then I am strong."*

2 Timothy 1:7 *"For God did not give us a spirit of timidity, but a spirit of power, of love and of self-discipline."*

Matthew 6:25 *"Therefore I tell you, do not worry about your life, what you will eat or drink; or about your body, what you will wear."*

Philippians 4:6-7 *"Do not be anxious about anything, but in every situation, by prayer and petition, with thanksgiving, present your requests to God. And the peace of God, which transcends all understanding, will guard your hearts and your minds in Christ Jesus."*

1 Peter 5:6-7 *"Humble yourselves, therefore, under God's mighty hand, that he may lift you up in due time. Cast all your anxiety on Him because he cares for you."*

When you feel discouraged

Psalm 55:22 *"Cast your cares on the Lord and He will sustain you; he will never let the righteous be shaken."*

2 Corinthians 4:16-18 *"Therefore we do not lose heart. Though outwardly we are wasting away, yet inwardly we are being renewed day by day. For our light and momentary troubles are achieving for us an eternal glory that far outweighs them all. So we fix our eyes not on what is seen, but on what is unseen, since what is seen is temporary, but what is unseen is eternal."*

When you are feeling tempted

1 Corinthians 10:13 *"No temptation has overtaken you except what is common to mankind. And God is faithful; he will not let you be tempted beyond what you can bear. But when you are tempted, He will also provide a way out so that you can endure it."*

1 Peter 1: 6-7 *"In this you greatly rejoice, though now for a little while you may have had to suffer grief in all kinds of trials. These have come so that your faith- of greater worth than gold, which perishes even though refined by fire – may be proved genuine and may result in praise, glory and honor when Jesus Christ is revealed."*

When you need forgiveness

Psalm 103:12 *"as far as the east is from the west, so far has he removed our transgressions from us."*

Colossians 3:13 *"Bear with each other and forgive one another if any of you has a grievance against someone. Forgive as the Lord forgave you."*

1 John 1:9 *"If we confess our sins, He is faithful and just and will forgive our sins and purify us from all unrighteousness."*

When you are grieving

Romans 8:38-39 *"For I am convinced that neither death nor life, neither angels nor demons, neither the present nor the future, nor any powers, neither height nor depth, nor anything else in all creation, will be able to separate us from the love of God that is in Christ Jesus our Lord."*

1 Thessalonians 4:13-18 *"Brothers, we do not want you to be ignorant about those who fall asleep, or to grieve like the rest of men, who have no hope. We believe that Jesus died and rose again and so we believe that God will bring with Jesus those who have fallen asleep in him. According to the Lord's own word, we tell you that we who are still alive, who are left till the coming of the Lord, will certainly not precede those who have fallen asleep. For the Lord himself will come down from heaven, with a loud command, with the voice of the archangel and with the trumpet call of God, and the dead in Christ will rise first. After that, we who are still alive and are left will be caught up together with them in the clouds to meet the Lord in the air. And so we will be with the Lord forever. Therefore encourage each other with these words."*

1 Peter 1:3-5 *"Praise be to the God and Father of our Lord*

Jesus Chris! In his great mercy he has given us new birth into a living hope through the resurrection of Jesus Chris from the dead, and into an inheritance that can never perish, spoil or fade. This inheritance is kept in heaven for you, who through faith are shielded by God's power until the coming of the salvation that is ready to be revealed in the last time."

Chapter 7

Single Parenting

Nothing really prepares a person for parenting. After marriage, most couples decide it's time to start a family. The planning and preparation that goes into having a child is exciting and a little stressful. When a couple gets pregnant, usually they imagine their life being spent together raising their kids, in a co-parent household. The baby showers are exciting because all your family and friends come together, showering you with gifts. Decorating the nursery is also another fun task on the pre-baby to-do list. I had envisioned a co-parent household for all of my children, until my life was turned upside down time and time again.

Single parenting is a whole new ballgame! With my first child, I wasn't fully prepared for parenting and I was even less prepared to be a single parent. My head was in four different directions on a daily basis with no one else's head to help. Between sports practices, volleyball games, basketball games, football games, cheerleading, track meets, softball and baseball games, school band and chorus concerts, homework, to the everyday grind of household chores, my head was spinning, barely able to keep up. All four of my children are still at home, and most days I'm also a referee embracing the chaos. I might not be the best multi-tasking single mom, but I wouldn't trade it for anything!

I ran across some material from a church pamphlet at my church that I keep close to my Bible. I'd like to share it with you because of how it validated me as well as reminded me of my priorities.

Dr. James Dobson calls single parenting "the toughest job in the universe." Few understand the loneliness and emotional hurt many single parents carry or how exhausting the role can be.

PRIORITY ONE: Keep your child's best in mind

Every parent is called to lay aside his or her own interests for children. That calling takes extra commitment when you're doing it alone. You may still be working through painful circumstances that led to becoming a solo parent, or dealing with an ex-spouse who is a negative influence on the children. Regardless of the emotions your specific circumstances may be causing, you are called to place your child's needs above your own. Give them as much stability and nurturing as you can. Providing stability includes doing your best to maintain a Christ-like attitude when you go through the headaches of court appointments, seeing your ex with a new romantic interest, juggling financial challenges, maintaining a home, or handling awkward questions about your family.

PRIORITY TWO: Choose good relationships

Few people understand the load you carry. You're likely to be under stress with extra work and the constant demands of parenting. You know how your loneliness and desire to be loved can lead you towards relationships with the opposite sex that may be harmful, only adding to the uncertainty and anxiety. If you are not ready to marry, be very cautious about dating during this season of life. You and your children need to be a part of a community of believers that will support you and help you navigate this season of your life.

PRIORITY THREE: Become intentional

You are a better parent than you think you are! Raising children alone is harder, but the goal is the same for you as it is for two parent families – to nurture Christian faith and values in your children. You must be intentional about building a strong relationship with your child, and modeling Godly character, and creating occasions for meaningful interaction about life's most important truths. God is eager to help you be the parent your children need. Written by Eastview Family Resources

This simple pamphlet was like gold to my heart. It was time for me to put myself in my children's shoes. They had seen and been through so much and I was determined to do things right this time. Taking the wrong path again wasn't an option. We all make mistakes because of our free will to make choices and sometimes those decisions are good and sometimes they're bad. We can choose to learn from life lessons or ignore them, most likely dooming us to repeat them. If we choose to make the same mistakes over and over again, we continue to exist without growth and make our lives harder than necessary.

Being stagnant wasn't my calling. I had dreams, goals,

ideas and motivation to become the best version of myself. We seem to reach out to God most when we hit rock bottom, but do we seek Him at the highest points in our lives? Do we thank Him enough? These were questions I was asking myself.

You could say I was extremely fearful of this next step in my life. *Who does God say I am? What does He want me to do with my life? Who does He want me in relationship with?* Noah St. John talks about fear in his book *The Secret Code of Success.* He says, "What causes the fear of asking? It's really the fear of rejection." That's exactly right. I had a fear of failing. I didn't want to fail as a mother and I didn't want to fail again as a wife, and I sure didn't want another man to fail me again. But when I made the decision to move forward on my own, being patient and focusing on God's plan for my life was my prayer every night.

I realized after listening to sermon after sermon, God wanted a relationship with me. Some people think it has to be formal. We don't have to be Bible scholars to have a relationship with the one and only God who loves us unconditionally. Reading the Bible is for everyone. Prayer is for everyone. Having a relationship with God is for everyone. Attending church is also for everyone. Unfortunately I've heard people say, "Everyone who attends church is a hypocrite." I always respond with, "We are all sinners, that's why we go to church." I so badly want those people to know what I know. My wish is for everyone to have the peace and grace God gives us each and every day.

Along with all my deep questions, I started to seek what God had in store for me. *What was I put on this earth to do? What special talents was I given? What are some positives about myself and what are the negatives about me that need some work?* Some new thoughts started emerging. *This horrible tragedy happened to my children and I seven years ago and I have the ability to help others through their losses, if I choose. I can either take that horrific moment in my life and dwell on it, or let it become something the Lord will use for good.*

It was at this moment I decided it was time to get my story down on paper.

Grieving? What is Grief?

Before I started writing this book, I had to look deep within myself to make sure I truly experienced grief. Was I healed? After I heard three different counselors say some version of, "I'm not sure if you've ever had a chance to grieve," I decided it was time to look into this *grieving* word everyone kept talking about. CS Lewis once said, "In the beginning of grief one wallows, screams, aches, cries, and feels so many levels of emptiness, but those expressions of grief are one's focus on the pain of the loss." That's exactly what I did when my husband died: focused on the emptiness and pain of the loss. That pain was huge. I tried to fill my emptiness with the wrong things. I still felt empty even though I thought life was going okay.

From family, to church friends, to strangers that hear my story for the first time, *grief* is a word mentioned quite often. So what is grief?

- Grief is the painful emotion of sorrow caused by the loss or impending loss of anyone or anything that has deep meaning to you.

- Grief begins in your heart as a natural response to a significant, unwanted loss.
- Grief is a God-given emotion that increases with knowledge about the sorrows of life. The wiser you are about the grief that people experience, the more you yourself will grieve.

—June Hunt, from her book called *Grief*

"With much wisdom comes much sorrow; the more knowledge, the more grief." (Ecclesiastes 1:18)

I learned that all people grieve differently. At first it was very difficult to be sad. Anger was the biggest emotion; angry at the mess I was dealing with. It was my burden to face all the problems he ran away from, along with being a single mom. Paperwork from attorneys buried me. I was trying to figure out how I could afford to take care of my children. I was just trying to keep my head above water, so grieving was the last thing on my mind. *Who has time for it?*

My immediate family didn't speak much about Chris unless it had to do with the litigation or answering someone's questions. On the other hand, close relatives of mine missed him terribly. They would express their feelings on social media throughout the years and talk about him as if he did nothing wrong. Everyone is entitled to their own opinions, but posting on social media how they missed him and how he was a great father and nephew was one of the most hurtful things for me. Maybe they didn't have all the sordid details I did.

My parents, my children and I were going through a catastrophic event involving the man I was married to, including the second life he hid from everyone. It's hard for me to comprehend how family could think to put anything positive about that man out there for the world to see, at least during that time. He cheated and lied his way through our marriage, possibly for years.

Another topic Jane Hunt talks about in her *Grief* book is chronic grief.

What is Chronic Grief?
- Chronic grief (or incomplete grief) is an unresolved, emotional sorrow experienced over a long period of time as the result of not accepting a significant loss or not experiencing closure of that loss.

"The troubles of my heart have multiplied; free me from my anguish." (Psalm 25:17)

- Chronic grief can also be an unresolved, deep sorrow experienced over a long period of time and characterized by misconceptions that result in failure to move through the grief process.

It's very possible I chose to ignore that word grief for the past seven years. Grief was something other people go through, not me. I never needed to grieve. I was moving on, I was stronger and I was surviving, at least I thought. Awareness is the first step toward progress. Knowing how to do something doesn't mean you *will* do it. Paul Martinelli says, "We will hit turbulence on our flight to a better fulfilled life. If we want to change our life, we have to change our programming. You either step forward into growth or backwards into comfort and safety."

It wasn't until March of 2018 that everything changed in an instant. God was giving me signs for years that I chose to ignore. I continued to mask my sorrow with relationships that weren't healthy for me. I was seeking happiness where happiness was only temporary. *Why did it take me so long to realize this? How different would my life be today if I would have followed a better path? Why couldn't I have been this wise years ago and not waste so much time?* Don't we all ask ourselves these questions? *What if, I wish this, I wish that, I regret this, I regret that...*

It's easy to look back and see all the what ifs, but I knew I couldn't continue to beat myself up. It's all a part of my journey and sometimes it takes some hardships to discover your true purpose.

Since childhood, music has always meant a lot to me. There is true beauty in music. Somehow, someway it always found a way to connect with me in my soul. The lyrics and instruments can be so incredibly moving.

My mother has been a music advocate for as long as I can remember. She instilled music in us from a young age and provided piano and trumpet lessons. She always said learning how to play the piano as a child was about learning how to read music. She would often remind us how music helps us with so many things in life. To this day my mom still participates in the pit band for school musicals, plays in a community band every summer, sings on the church praise team and sings and plays the trumpet for the Easter cantatas at church. I'm so thankful for her music passion.

Listening to Christian radio was something I didn't do regularly, and even less after he died. . Chris would always listen to Christian radio stations in his vehicle. I remember getting into his SUV several times and our local station 91.7 would be on. Sunday was my Christian music day, but rarely ever listened during the week. Pop and Country music were always my first choice, with the Christian praise and worship songs being my last pick.

After his funeral, it took me several years to be able to listen to any praise and worship songs in my car. After I found a new church, I was drawn into more of the modern Christian songs. I soon became a big fan of Pandora's Chris Tomlin Radio, Jesus Culture Radio and even Hymns 4 Worship Radio. I enjoyed the mix of modern praise songs, along with old Hymns from my childhood.

One of the songs that has played a huge role in my healing process is "O Come to the Altar" by Elevation Worship. Look it up if you have a moment and see if it blesses you as much as it has me. It sings of how Jesus calls us despite our brokenness and sin, and we can come to His open arms. Regrets, sorrow and mistakes can be traded for joy and new life.

I sang this song so many times and tears would fill my eyes every time. Sometimes, the song would distract me from what I was doing and I would pause, turn up the volume, allow my heart to melt as I worshipped, then continue on with cooking, cleaning or whatever task I'd been doing. Other times, I couldn't let myself go to that spiritual place because I was struggling with decisions in my life. Over the years, during praise and worship time at church, I would hear the transition shift from one song into "O Come to the Altar" and would shut down.

Memories of My Childhood

I have fond, childhood memories of sitting in the old wooden pews every Sunday morning, dressed in my Sunday best, opening up the Hymn books and singing "The Old Rugged Cross" and "Amazing Grace" to the pipe organ and piano. Our Sunday morning routine growing up is cemented in my memory. As much as my sister Rene and I despised the words from my mother, "Girls, time to get up for Sunday school" every week at 8:00 a.m., we weren't given a choice. We got up and attended church as a family. We grew up knowing that we would go to heaven if we asked Jesus to come into our hearts. So I remember praying to God around the age of five asking Him to come into my heart over and over again. I would ask the next night and the next night. I wanted to make sure He heard me so I could go to heaven where the streets are gold with pearly gates.

My sister and I didn't realize it at that time, but the consistent, routine Christian values and morals my parents instilled in us at a very young age would carry us in our adult lives. As a mother, raising children in a totally different type of world, I'm so thankful for what my parents did for me.

I soon realized good friends of mine (and guys I dated)

didn't grow up with that same routine. It took many years for me to see that what children grow up with in their homes is considered their "normal." The weekly routine in my home growing up was very different than what I learned about others' experiences. That made dating very difficult for me, which is why I became immediately interested in Chris when I learned about his upbringing.

I often look back to my childhood and think, *wow, if I only knew what was going to happen to me at the age of 32.* God gave me the strongest, most honest and loyal parents anyone could ever want. He also blessed me with my sister, Rene, my best friend forever. I can't imagine being born into any other family and surviving a tragedy like this. My family was so pure and perfect to me as a child. My parents were diligent servants of the Lord, highly involved in the church. They both were raised in Christian homes as well. They lived by the Ten Commandments every day and had hopes my sister and I would always do the same.

The Ten Commandments
1. I am the Lord your God: you shall not have strange Gods before me
2. Thou shall not take the name of the Lord your God in vain
3. Remember to keep holy the Lord's Day
4. Honor your father and mother
5. You shall not kill
6. You shall not commit adultery
7. You shall not steal
8. You shall not bear false witness against your neighbor
9. You shall not covet your neighbor's wife

10. You shall not covet your neighbor's goods.

We honored the Lord's day unlike anyone else I knew. It was a day of rest, so after church and lunch, we either played outside or rested inside. We never worked on that day, we couldn't even mow the lawn or wash our cars on Sundays. That is all I ever knew, so those habits continued on into my adult years until I started to develop my own ways. Sunday was still a day of rest, but I took it as "family day." Sundays are very sacred to me. If we don't start the day off with church, then my entire week is off course.

Kids are being raised in a world full of technology and social media, and cyber bullying and school shootings are way too frequent. It's a scary world they are growing up in. I try to get my kids to understand it's not necessary to be in every single extra-curricular activity that exists for their ages. It's too much; too much busyness and pressure. Kids are faced with challenges we didn't face 35 years ago. Yes, families had different types of problems then, but the amount of pressure on children these days saddens me. It's so easy to be on the go constantly. There are too many opportunities to be busy, spinning your wheels, not necessarily doing anything impactful or significant. Finding the time to sit down together at the dinner table at home to enjoy a home-cooked meal, carry-out or delivery is a priority to me. The conversation that takes place around the table doesn't compare to other talks throughout the day.

The most common phrase I've heard in the past ten

years is, "I just don't have time." I hear that on a daily basis at work, from friends, etc., so I try my hardest to only use that line when I absolutely do not have one extra minute in my day. I know I make the time for things I truly want to do. It's human nature to put off the things we don't feel like doing.

A couple of things people most commonly put on the back burner are exercise and reading, whether it be an email, kid's homework, a novel or the Bible. I was told years ago that we are no different tomorrow other than the people we meet and the books we read. Wow. That's an eye-opening statement. In regards to exercise, our bodies were designed to move! I advise my clients to make workouts a daily priority, just like showering and brushing their teeth. You will often hear from me, "We are only given one earthly body so treat it well."

Parenting is one of the most difficult things I've ever done, but knowing it's hard makes me want to be better. Building a strong foundation, a loving home centered around God is what I strive for the most. If we put God in the center, everything else should fall into place at the right time. God loved us so much that He sent his own son to die on the cross for our sins so we can spend eternity with Him in heaven. Jesus sacrificing Himself is the most loving act anyone could ever think about doing. God's own son, Jesus Christ, hung on the cross to die for our sins because of His great love for us. Why would we not follow God's advice? How could anyone choose not to believe in Him, I wonder? I had to keep reminding myself that this foundational belief was "my normal."

From past experience, most of my friends weren't aware of this blessing, and it was my responsibility to share with them.

"He said to them, "Go into all the world and preach the good news to all creation. Whoever believes and is baptized will be saved, but whoever does not believe will be condemned."
(Mark 15:15-16)

Although I wanted to share and teach, I never wanted to be a preachy person. But, having witnessed God's love, guidance and protection in so many situations in my past, I no longer want to be hesitant to let people know about His goodness. I have been afraid people would reject me. *Why would I jeopardize losing friends? How would I even begin that conversation with someone?* But I have come to realize what I have to say could change a person's life. *Why should I hide what He's done for me?* I decided to put more faith in the Lord to help me figure it out and to let go of my pride.

"For pride is a spiritual cancer; it eats up the very possibility of love, contentment, or even common sense." – C.S. Lewis

I think back and wonder if Chris had too much pride. Maybe he could have reached out to someone before he got in way over his head. How would things be different today if he had?

When pride comes, then comes disgrace, but with humility, comes wisdom. (Proverbs 11:2)

Chapter 8

Kristin's Broken Heart

Kristin heard the words "Chris has been shot" at the very same time I learned about the tragedy. She was an innocent five-year-old kindergartener who adored her daddy. Kristin was a daddy's girl from the day she was born. They had an inseparable bond that was apparent to everyone. I treasure the adorable photos of Chris and Kristin in their matching Chicago Cubs t-shirts or Chicago Bears attire. They attended a mission's trip together for our church a year before he died. Taking a four-year-old on a mission's trip definitely takes patience, and Chris had all the patience in the world for her. A child that age can't do a whole lot to help out on a trip like that, but he thought it would be a good experience for her. Whenever we went boating, she was always driving the boat on Daddy's lap. He taught her all about fishing, camping and fixing food over a campfire. Basically anything adults could do, Chris would let Kristin chime along with him. Their sweet father-daughter bond was so deep, Kristin's heart was completely broken the day she heard the news.

My other two children didn't have as much reaction since they were so young. I remember when James got home from daycare that afternoon and I had to tell him the devastating news. He came up and hugged me and I said to him, "Hey buddy, I want to talk to you about something," and he just stared at me with his baby blue eyes when I said, "Daddy won't be coming back home." The precious look he gave me broke my heart. I don't think his three-year-old little mind understood what I was saying. I just told him that Daddy went to heaven to be with Jesus so he wouldn't be coming back home again. He immediately ran into the master bedroom and laid on the floor of Chris' side of the bed. That moment broke my heart into another million pieces. I had no idea how to handle this situation. Obviously this was a first for me. I was trying to keep it together for my kids, so helping them through it was first on my mind.

After Chris's death, we finished out Kristin's dance year. I no longer had the time or the finances to afford to keep her in competitive dance. Even being there in that dance building was too difficult for me to cope with, so taking some time off from dance was okay for both of us. Chris was very involved in Kristin's dance life. He would often take her to lessons when I was home with the other kids or vice versa. At the time, Kristin was also dealing with kids at school making comments to her about her dad. It was a very awkward time for a five-year-old.

Because she was only five years old when she lost her father, the sting will forever be present. Kristin began talking with school counselors to try and sort out her feelings, then she started seeing a Christian counselor who was recommended to us. Kristin never wanted to discuss with me what she relayed to her counselor and I was okay with that. I just felt thankful she was willing to talk with someone trustworthy about her feelings. Her journey of grief and healing was full of heartache and I needed to be understanding.

The other children weren't experiencing the same grief and confusion Kristin was. James was only three years old and Norah was turning one when their father died. Sadly, Norah doesn't remember her father except for what she sees in photo albums.

Talking positively about their father was something I couldn't do for years. If they felt the need to ask questions or make comments about him, I would answer truthfully, but never elaborated on anything more. Things changed after the divorce. Finally I felt like we could discuss Chris as we needed to without being reprimanded. While I was married, I was told several times that I just need to *get over it*. Joe would say, "Everyone needs to quit babying those kids." That was so hurtful to me, so I would clam up. I believed at the time that I needed to respect the man I was married to, so I tried to shut down and silence that part of my broken heart.

We only visited the cemetery twice after Chris died. One time I remember getting the kids ice cream and then taking a drive to build up the nerve to take them to their Dad's grave site. I wasn't prepared for their questions, so I stalled as long as possible. The cemetery was a place I felt the need to just ignore all together, but my drive to work three days a week took me right past it. There were days I would tell myself *don't look to the left* as I passed by, but nonetheless my head would turn, catching a glimpse of his headstone. His grave site just happened to be one of the few closest to the main road. Sometimes I would squint my eyes to see if I noticed any new flowers or plaques around his grave site. *Has anyone dropped flowers by? Is the plaque on the easel still standing from the funeral? Is the little angel from one of the flower arrangements still sitting along the base of the headstone?*

Finally, on the six-year anniversary of his death, I took the kids by his grave for the first time in years. It was something I'd planned for a couple months, knowing that date was approaching. We placed some purple flowers there and read the back of his head stone.

"For God so loved the world that he gave His only begotten Son, that whoever believes in him shall not perish but have eternal life." (John 3:16)

It was bone-chilling weather, so we quickly returned to the car and went home. The kids didn't ask any questions that evening, but in the days and weeks following, something changed: more joy emerged. It's like we broke the barrier of deprivation that day. We were able to talk about Chris with a better perspective. My kids saw me smile when I told them how they reminded me of him.

I continued to remind the kids of the fun things we used to do with their dad. They already knew he was an avid Chicago Cubs and Chicago Bears fan. On our Christmas tree each year, we continued to hang a Chicago Bears ornament in remembrance of Chris.

Over the years I noticed Kristin just wasn't the same carefree little girl she was when her Daddy was still alive. Watching her demeanor at the dinner table or watching her communicate with friends, I could always see a lingering sadness in the back of her eyes. Some days I wondered if I could ever be enough for her. I will never be able to replace her father, but I'm trying to be all she needs. I've told my kids repeatedly that there may not be a man in the house, but God is our Father and our helper.

Kristin wrote in a journal from time to time. Writing things down was recommended from one of her counselors. I journaled for years and found it very beneficial. Writing thoughts and feelings down on paper was (and still is) a release, a way of feeling better at the end of the day. It has also been a good way to evaluate from year to year how far we've come over time.

One of the pieces from Kristin's journal reads:

TRUST

When I heard that my dad was gone forever, I didn't know what to think. I just started crying. As I've grown up more and really thought about it, I realized that NO ONE will ever be able to replace my dad. I walk into a restaurant and see a dad and his daughter sitting by each other laughing or when I see daddy daughter dances, it all makes me think...I will never have that again even if my mom remarries because it just won't be the same. But, in the end I remind myself that God has His reasons. Yes, I may not understand His reasoning, but God knows and understands it, so we just have to trust that God will help us through whatever comes our way.

Sincerely,
Kristin

Kristin and Chris walking to the car after her dance recital

How Chris is Remembered

Year after year, I would receive emails or Facebook messages from people remembering Chris around the anniversary date of his death. One year I received a card from a soccer mom of a boy who attended Camp Shutout in Birmingham Alabama. Chris was a goalie coach at that camp for over 12 years. Every summer he took a week off of work, drove up to Alabama University and coached soccer players to become better goalies. He was enthusiastic about the sport and loved to coach the kids. In August 2017, I received a card that read:

"My son was honored to receive the Chris Randall Award at Camp Shutout this year. Many coaches told him that this was the best award anyone could get. Several coaches came up to me to tell me how much of an accomplishment this award is and how proud I should be if my son is like Chris. I just wanted you to know the impact Chris has had on the soccer community. It was such a meaningful day; so meaningful that our family is donating to start a Camp Shutout Scholarship in Chris' name. Wishing you all the best!"

I was happy, sad, thankful and amazed to see the legacy Chris left behind at Camp Shutout. That card was exactly what I needed to see in order to start seeing Chris in a more positive light again.

Today we continue to talk about Chris in our daily happenings. The kids smile when I notice how something they do or an expression they make is so similar to their father's. They enjoy hearing about their dad, because as far as they know, he was perfect to them. He loved them during the short time he had with them. The fond memories of him will forever be treasured in their precious little minds.

A friend of mine said, "I genuinely believe Chris realized a side of him he didn't like; the side the devil had control of. But he didn't know how to break away and be free. You made him realize there is love in the world. Unfortunately he chose the wrong way, but God didn't abandon him. Chris stuck around because he felt trapped. Chris was a part of your path to a much bigger purpose. Your path was paved long before you came into this world. If God brings you to it, He will bring you through it."

"I know the plans that I have for you", declares the Lord.
(Jeremiah 29:11)

Chapter 9

Time Does Heal – Post-Traumatic Stress

At the time of the loss, the last thing I wanted to hear from people was "everything happens for a reason" or "time heals." I believed that for everyone else but myself. *If Chris committing suicide happened for a reason, it wasn't a good one.* I'm not sure if some of my friends and family quite understood exactly what I was living out day by day for four years straight. Usually when someone passes away, it's extremely sad, people grieve, and then start the healing process right away. My situation was much different. My husband died and the shock filled the community for weeks, but what no one really knows is the extra, oppressive aftermath. A tragic death, yes, but also followed by attorney visits, lawsuits, courthouse visits and depositions and troublesome revelations. While in the middle of lawsuits and trials, I couldn't see the light at the end of the tunnel. Deep in my heart I trusted God had some sort of plan for me, but that rarely came out of my mouth.

The fact is, some people grieve and heal faster than others. Every loss is different from the next. We have no idea what people are dealing with following their loved one's death. No one ever truly gets over the loss, it changes a person. But we will get stronger, and if we have faith, then we're wise enough to know we're safe in the arms of God. Yes I had all the normal feelings after the loss of my husband: shock, anger and confusion for several years after he died. I also felt extremely rejected. How worthless I felt was something I never verbalized. It's no wonder – I was married to someone who had a secret life. Lying to and cheating on me no doubt caused rejection to blanket my soul. *Why wasn't our marriage and family enough to keep him here? Since when did he start making those immoral and illegal decisions that would cause his demise?*

I went through a whirlwind of emotions for years and to this day, some things are still difficult to think about. The nightmares, the flashbacks, difficulty concentrating and social withdraws I have from time to time are a result of the trauma. I never allowed myself to say I was suffering from post-traumatic stress, but I had so many symptoms on that list.

I suffered recurring nightmares in the beginning. One specific dream I can't seem to erase from my memory happened early on. In the dream we were still living in the golf course home, and the kids and I were playing in the family room, enjoying a normal evening at home. Off in the corner window was Chris standing outside on the deck, just looking in on us with a very empty look on his face. It's like he just appeared to see that his children were doing okay. I was the only one who noticed him standing there. I woke up very startled. Seeing him in that dream wasn't scary to me, it created an interesting sense of satisfaction that I hadn't felt since before his death. It left me with a thought that *maybe Chris can really see us from heaven. Maybe God isn't the only one watching over us. Maybe it's true when people say their loved ones are watching over them from above.* Maybe. I chose to believe it's possible because it was so difficult for me to think Chris would never see his beautiful and talented children ever again, until we all are reunited in eternity.

On a daily basis, I still experience flashbacks. The memories we had together with our children were wonderful. Chris was a fun-loving, spontaneous, adventurous guy who loved to entertain. I can't go on a vacation and not think about Chris. He was the first to book airline tickets to Florida to visit his parents a couple times a year or take a trip on a cruise ship. Chris also enjoyed taking long 3-day weekends to do something fun. He sure knew how to plan a football tailgate party and he never went small. Attending any sporting events takes me back to all the fun times we went to Chicago for a game or when he took me to my first NFL game ever: the Chicago Bears vs. the Green Bay Packers. Chris always chose the best of the best tickets, no matter the price. We sat seven rows back from the corner of the end zone. What an experience for my first NFL game! The very last Cubs game we attended together was two years before he died. Those seats were just five rows behind home plate! WOW! He really knew how to make memories that would last a lifetime.

There are many days when I had difficulty concentrating. I had so much to process after Chris died, it was like a thick fog swallowed up my time. Days and weeks ran together. A few months after Chris died, I attended a school open house for my nieces, where a little girl came up to me out of nowhere and said, "Hey, didn't your husband just die?" I felt like someone kicked me hard in the stomach. I wasn't sure how to respond, but uttered, "Um, yes that's me." The little girl just went on talking to my nieces, while I looked around to see if anyone else had heard that, or if I was imagining it. Kids do say the darndest things, so I quickly brushed that off. However, that didn't fully prepare me for the public humiliation that was to come.

I had to be strong for my children, so I somehow waded my way through the weeks and months. I found myself apologizing to people for interrupting them or having to tell my kids to repeat what they asked me. With the weight of the world on my shoulders, my mind didn't ever shut off. I was constantly planning and preparing for the future. My mother would tell me, "Casey, that's years away, why worry about that now?" I wasn't prepared for the tragic news that January day, so I did everything I was physically capable of doing to prepare for what might happen next. *Certainly another tragedy is on its way.* Some people have said that my presumptuous planning for the worst might have been caused by post-traumatic stress. *Post-traumatic stress? Isn't that just for military service members and war survivors?* I would never admit I had some post-traumatic stress indications going on in my day to day life.

The week I started finding out about his lies, I started taking down picture frames and removing anything in sight that reminded me of him. I avoided songs on the radio for years. I sold our bedroom set because I had no sentimental attachment to it. I pawned my wedding ring because it no longer had meaning. To this day, I don't regret purging and tucking things away. At the time, I felt as though my life was a joke.

Depression or Anxiety Throughout the Years

After the loss of my husband, I wasn't sure if I was suffering from bouts of depression or maybe exaggerated anxiety...or both. My anxiety had definitely reached its peak, but I was able to function. *I can function, so I can't be depressed, right?* Post-partum depression cleared up and was no longer a concern of mine after my divorce. Anxiety showed up in things like how paranoid I was about something bad happening to my children. I was worried about getting in a car accident with them in the car. I didn't want my kids walking anywhere, because I'd seen too many kidnapping stories on the news, I didn't want them shopping with me, because I wouldn't be able to take my eyes off of them and actually shop. I didn't want my kids playing outside without an adult, even though they were old enough to do so. Even thoughts like *am I healthy enough? Will they lose me too?* I started taking better care of my health, knowing I'm the only parent they have left.

During my second marriage, I had reoccurring thoughts, wondering if someone would be knocking on my front door to deliver more bad news. *Your second husband won't be coming back home, either...* Those worries of mine were heightened to the extreme! It was time for me to get some help. My counselor told me over and over again I had symptoms of PTSD.

Recovering from Chris' death on my own was one thing, but to recover with three small children was emotionally draining. Then to add a dating relationship on top of that, I was completely camouflaging the whole grieving process. I never took the time needed to adjust to my situation.

So, after seven years went by with one failed marriage and one broken relationship, the heavy cloud was starting to lift. Sure, I still had days I didn't get out of my sweatpants or brush my hair, getting through doing the bare minimum, which was caring for my kids. Some days the thought of leaving the house to go anywhere with small children wore me out. I started going to work without doing my hair or make-up. I wasn't making time for myself in the mornings or afternoons, or ever really. My oldest daughter said to me many times, "Gosh Mom, all you want to do is sit around the house." *What happened to the fun outgoing person I once was? Did a part of me die when I lost Chris? Am I not a fun mom anymore?*

Having another adult around to share the responsibility would have been great, but that wasn't reality. It was just me. I had to figure out how to run the household without losing my mind.

My sister and I grew up with chores in order to earn an allowance. We weren't allowed to touch the laundry, but we had to keep up on our short list of daily chores. I never wanted my kids to feel like I was making them slave away, but I learned the responsibility of chores could benefit them in the future. I had to look at it

124

differently. Teaching them instead of *putting them to work* was the goal, because learning responsibility is a good thing. Someday they'll each have homes and families of their own to take care of, so it was time for me to ask them to help.

Honestly, I needed their help with chores, but had to let go of thinking everything needed to be done to perfection. After a few lessons on laundry and housework, I would catch them bringing up their own bed sheets, or their laundry hampers to start a load all by themselves. *Nice work!* Keeping up with laundry for five people when there is school plus a busy sports calendar is tough! Now, we all sit down together and fold laundry while we watch a TV show, almost like sitting around the dinner table telling good stories. Believe it or not, our laundry time is quality time together. I couldn't believe our household was operating so much better! The kids started making their own scrambled eggs, grilled cheese sandwiches, peanut butter and jelly, ramen noodles, and even loaded and unloaded the dishwasher. A child that likes to cook and clean makes a mom happy!

Some Final Thoughts and Encouragement for My Readers

Chapter 10

My Inspirational Turning Point

Inspirational Moment

One late night, driving home at 9:00 p.m. in a snow storm with four chatty, energetic children wasn't exactly how I envisioned Easter would wrap up in central Illinois. I parked the car in the garage, getting out of the five inches of snow covering the neighborhood, get all the kids inside, and the whole time I'm thinking *wow, this single parenting thing is exhausting. It would be nice if someone could share this responsibility with me, but I can do this. God is giving me the focus I need now and I'm not going to let Him down.*

Pushing through, I put my toddler to bed in her crib, directed the other kids to head to bed, and then went back to the garage to unload the trunk full of groceries and Easter basket goodies. Snow covered my tail lights and license plate. Some Easter! As I made a couple trips back and forth, something was telling me to get to my computer and write. I had a story that needed to be told.

Before I sat down at my computer, I went around my house, opening cabinets and nightstand drawers, and pulled out all the books I'd read in the past few years; the books that have impacted me the most. I joined a health and wellness company in the fall of 2015, and every few months we had a book study. Basically it was like our business, goal-setting and mindset homework. We'd read a certain amount of chapters every few weeks. Little did I know while I was reading them that those helpful books would help me become the person I am today.

It was at that moment God was telling me something. That saying I've heard all my life: "when one door closes, another one opens" went through my mind. Typically that phrase is murmured by people who either lose a job or get their hearts broken. We've all probably heard that phrase at some point in our lives, but do we ever really pay attention to how it plays out? I finally did! Looking back, *yes, I see it.* I could see how one job led to the next, how one business opportunity lead to the next, how one broken relationship ended and the next one began, how each person I met along my journey connected me to the next open door, etc. They were *all* stepping stones. *I'm still going somewhere, thank God.* I immediately prayed, "Thank you, Lord. Thank you for the clarity You've given me. Thank you for giving me the focus I need for myself and for my children, Amen."

I have witnessed some heartaches and other tragedies around me over the years, but the one hitting closest to home took place in the spring of 2018. My former Youth Pastor, Dan, lost his 29-year-old son in a tragic car accident in March of 2018. His son, Jeff, had just spoken at church the Sunday before, announcing his new media job in the mission field. Jeff was a shy kid, a great person with a beautiful heart. He was driving home after praise team practice on a Thursday night and went to turn left on a road a mile from his house, when a car came up from behind, smashing into the driver's door. When you hear a story like this, you wonder *WHY?* Why would Jeff's life be taken so early? What is the purpose of this tragedy? During these kinds of confusing times, we must turn to the Lord in prayer. Only God knows why, and when we have great faith, we have the strength to get through anything. Sometimes *WHY* is where we get stuck.

Many choose to be angry with God when something like this happens. *John 10:10 says "The thief's purpose is to steal and kill and destroy. My purpose is to give them a rich and satisfying life."* So as we can see, the thief (Satan) is always out to destroy anything that is good.

When I drove over to Pastor Dan's house that following morning, he welcomed me with, "Thank you for coming, Casey. God is still good." Those words are forever embedded in my mind. Jeff's own father, a man of great faith, just lost his son and he told me that God is still good. Powerful.

Changing for the Better

This past year has been eye-opening for me. During my soul searching, I realized things I used to enjoy weren't fulfilling anymore. *Were they ever truly fulfilling or were they just used as a crutch to get through whatever I was going through at the time?* For example, going out with friends, having a few cocktails and trying to enjoy the nightlife was getting old after so many years. *This is lame.* I never had the kind of parents who engaged in the party scene, so maybe my homegrown roots were starting to come through. Maybe it had to do with age or being a mom. Or maybe it had to do with being convicted in my faith. For years I was bored and unentertained while trying to enjoy the nightlife away from my kids. I tried it anyway, thinking I'd like it again someday. Concerts weren't as enjoyable anymore, parties were boring, small town gatherings that used to be fun were very unappealing to me. There was a restlessness I couldn't explain. I was being moved towards something.

My entire life I had played tug of war between doing things my way and doing what I knew was right. Having a free will can be tough. God didn't promise us life on earth would be simple. Actually, we have a responsibility as Christians to be a good example to others. Was I a good example to my friends in college? No! Was I a good example in my early 20's trying to make it as a working adult? Not really! Was I becoming a better example after my first born child? Yes, finally! We get wiser the older we get.

I was very weak as a 20-year-old college girl. I *knew* what was right, but I chose to do life my way, because I thought it was more fun. Living on the edge seemed more appealing in my early 20s. Unfortunately that lifestyle left me with a guilty conscious time and time again. I used to go out with friends on campus almost every Saturday night, only to wake up the next morning and drive 30 minutes to church with a headache. I would make it to church, just so my family could see I was living a good life. Was I really? Heck no! I concealed the party side of me, only to the general public, figuring as long as I made it to church every Sunday morning, I was still being a good Christian girl. Little did I know, I was falling short of God's best for me each and every week.

"For all have sinned and fall short of the glory of God."
(Romans 3:23)

It took me a few years to grow out of that stage. The party scene wasn't worth feeling tired and worthless most weekends. I valued my health way too much to keep that routine any longer.

When people complain about getting older, I look at it as a blessing. We all start out as innocent children who mind our parents, yet disobey often. We get in trouble and the cycle continues. As young children, we don't always choose our thoughts – they're chosen for us by our parents, teachers and other influences around us. We turn into young adults with a free will and responsibilities, and real life gets scary! Our belief systems morph based on experiences we go through. Then we mature into wiser people, contributing to society and caring about what goes on in the world. Every passing year leads to more life experiences. It's a journey to greater wisdom.

"The only source of wisdom is experience." — Albert Einstein

Embracing who you are is very important, and if you can do it at a young age, you are in good shape for adulthood. So many people choose to conform to peer pressure that exists everywhere, rather than discovering who they are. Life as a teenager is challenging, and I pray my children get through high school and college being the unique, wonderful individuals God created them to be.

As a child, I was one of *those* kids…always thinking my parents didn't know what they were talking about. Looking back, I can admit they were the smartest, most loving people in my life. They wanted the best for me from the first day I was born, but as a teenager, I didn't appreciate what they were trying to do.

Living through the tragic event of my husband's suicide followed by four years of lawsuits and litigation, my parents still proved to be the most loving, caring people I knew. You'd think losing my husband and the subsequent lawsuits would have been the worst struggle I would ever have. But, strangely, I found that wasn't going to be my longest-lasting struggle in life. The tragedy recovery was temporary; a temporary time period because I learned it was a choice I had to make. I could choose to walk in misery, dwelling on my past or choose to move forward with a whole new outlook on life.

Walking a good path in my faith has been my longest standing life struggle. Growing up, I believed in God, I believed in Jesus Christ and I believed the Bible to be true. Even though I lived the routine life of attending church, Sunday school, youth group, Bible school and Christian summer camps, I never fully *absorbed* the Bible. I would let the Bible stories go in one ear and out the other. I attended Sunday school and Wednesday night youth group because my parents didn't give me a choice. Was I happy about it at the time? No. Am I thankful now for the strong foundation they built for my sister and I? Yes.

Some of it soaked in.

I often heard people say all of life's answers are found in the Bible. Well, I had my own way of thinking. I mostly believed that phrase, even though I opened my Bible maybe five times in ten years. Regretfully, I was ashamed that over half of my life was spent in church three times a week learning about God's Word and I didn't grasp more than I did. *Where did I go wrong?* Instead of focusing on where I went wrong, I started to appreciate what my parents did for me. Because of their modeling, I am raising my kids the same way. Having God in the center of our lives, helps everything around Him make more sense. I am forever grateful to my mom and dad for establishing a solid, loving family life focused around the one and only God.

"Start children off on the way they should go, and even when they are old they will not turn from it." (Proverbs 22:6)

Is Your FAITH Bigger than Your FEAR?

I was contemplating a new job after my second marriage ended. I was stressed, fearful and wasn't quite sure I was making the right decision. *Am I making the right decision? What if I fail? What will people think of me?* Then someone said to me, "Your faith has to be bigger than your fear." A light bulb went on immediately after she spoke those words. I had been through a horrible period in my life that had me questioning *everything;* everything about myself, about my life, about my faith and about my future, and I came out stronger than ever. I was positive I had great faith at that point.

"It's an interesting thing about fear; we put total faith in it. We feel that something is going to happen and we trust that implicitly. We allow it to control our thinking, our feeling and our actions...and therefore, our results." — Roddy Galbraith

I knew what I had to do in order to be confident that a new job was right for me: PRAY! I always heard stories from other people who claimed they knew when God was telling them to do something specific, but I never encountered moments like that with God. If I did, I never gave Him the credit. *God, are You speaking to me? Please help me hear.* We pray because God commands us to pray. We pray in preparation for major decisions.

"Do not be anxious about anything, but in every situation, by prayer and petition, with thanksgiving, present your requests to God." (Philippians 4:6-7)

"And it came to pass in those days, that he went out into a mountain to pray, and continued all night in prayer to God." (Luke 6:12)

I heard Charles Stanley speak about hearing from God on my drive to work one day. Charles Stanley is the senior pastor of the First Baptist Church in Atlanta, Georgia, and founder and president of In Touch Ministries. He said, "Everyone wants God to answer their prayers immediately. What they don't realize is that they are missing the personal relationship with the One and only God who loves us unconditionally." That made perfect sense to me. When we focus on the Lord, we have a sense of peace that comes over us. We gain patience and understanding, knowing His timing is best. That doesn't mean we have to like the waiting game, but being a faithful follower of Jesus Christ means we are putting our trust in Him. He has our best interests in mind.

"When we do His will in His way with His help, no one and nothing can stand in the way of our success. The key is seeking the presence of the Lord." —Charles Stanley

Do You Believe?

Do you feel like you've made too many mistakes and God won't forgive you? Do you keep repeating the same mistake over and over again? Do you wish things were different in your life? Do you feel uncomfortable walking in to a church? Maybe you feel like you don't fit in. Have you spent a majority of your life feeling lonely or ashamed? Many people feel this way. In fact, most people I talk to about faith, feel that way.

We are all sinners, even those who attend church. The only perfect being who walked this earth was the Son of God, Jesus Christ. Romans 3:23 says, *"for all have sinned and fall short of the glory of God"*

Romans 12:1-2 says, *"And do not be conformed to this world, but be transformed by the renewing of your mind, so that you may prove what the will of God is, that which is good and acceptable and perfect. Therefore I urge you, brethren, by the mercies of God to present your bodies a living and holy sacrifice, acceptable to God, which is your spiritual service of worship."* Does this resonate with you?

Chapter 11

Hills and Valleys

As we get older, it's inevitable: we've all experienced some sort of significant loss in our lives. The pain we go through with grieving and healing is sometimes life-long, but we can make our path easier by making the choice to believe in a Loving Heavenly Father. Charles Stanley said, "The depth of the valley will determine what God is able to accomplish in our life." I believe the deepest valley I experienced was the death of my husband and the four years that followed. During that time, my parents made it very clear to me what my two choices were: either choose to respond poorly to this disaster or hold my head up and know God is walking along side, all the way through.

The only thing we can control is how we respond to certain situations. God knows our thoughts, our stubbornness and our habits. We can't hide anything from Him, because He knows our every move before we even think about what it will be. He wants the best for us. He might take us down a deep valley in order for us to reconnect with Him, but it will all be worth it. It took tragedy and a toxic marriage for me to make things right with myself and the Lord.

"Even though I walk through the darkest valley, I will fear no evil, for you are with me; your rod and your staff, they comfort me." (Psalm 23:4)

You might be thinking *what does God's rod and staff have to do with comforting me?* That doesn't mean He's out to get you or punish you. It's not His whippin' stick. Picture a shepherd and his sheep. The shepherd uses a rod to discipline the sheep and a staff to direct them. If the sheep is headed off the cliff, the shepherd uses his rod and staff to redirect the sheep, steering them in the right direction. As parents we do the same thing. If our children are making bad decisions, we discipline them and redirect them. So when you're headed down the wrong path, God will bring discipline and direction in your life to keep you from veering away onto slippery slopes. It's comforting to know somebody loves me enough to tell me when I'm going the wrong way.

Those valleys we go through can teach us so much when our eyes are open to learn. We are more apt to pray and ask for help when we feel lonely or when we lose something of significance, or when our friends turn their backs on us or when we get that bad news from the doctor. Do we thank God when everything is wonderful though, when we have the big house, the fancy car, when everything is going our way? Being on the mountain top isn't when we need God the most, but those are the times to show our gratefulness the most. Sometimes the valleys are created to get us to stop and realize we are off path. Following God's will for our lives is when He can truly bless us to the fullest. His paths drip with abundance.

God wants a personal relationship with each and every one of us. From a very young age, I was told to make decisions as if God was in the same room with me, whether it be at school, in the car or sitting in my own living room. He loves us no matter what we do, but He wants to be involved in every decision we make. You might think that is a little much, but it's true. Think about all the times you've made irrational, spur-of-the-moment decisions, resulting in mistakes. Maybe it was a financial loss or maybe it was a loss of a meaningful relationship. There are things we regret in life, wishing we would have done things differently or taken a day to sleep on it. Some of you might think hindsight is 20/20, but knowing that is enough to make me want to slow down, be more rational and pray for guidance first. Again, this is where wisdom and patience come into play. The older we get, our life experiences help us to make better choices.

Charles Stanley encouraged me to respond like this...

1. Surrender your life to God.
2. Believe that God will use the valley experience for something good. If we could see what God sees, then we would ask Him to send us to the valley.

"And we know that in all things God works for the good of those who love him, who have been called according to his purpose." (Romans 8:28)

3. Rest in his wisdom, love and power.
4. Thank God for bringing us through the valley. Valley's make us more useful to God. Since He allowed it, it's the best way for Him to accomplish His purpose.

139

When I read, "If we could see what God sees from the mountaintop, then we would ask Him to send us to the valley," it made so much sense. I came to the conclusion that seven years later, I'm able to tell my story from a place of strength. Writing this book was part of my healing journey, but most of all, God gave me the strength to complete it. I'm able to share with you the tragic event that took me down the darkest, most lonely valley I've ever experienced. But God was walking by my side the entire time. What came to mind is the beautiful poem *Footprints in the Sand*, written by Mary Fishback Powers.

One night I dreamed a dream.
As I was walking along the beach with my Lord,
Across the dark sky flashed scenes from my life.
For each scene, I noticed two sets of footprints in the sand,
One belonging to me and one to my Lord.

After the last scene of my life flashed before me,
I looked back at the footprints in the sand.
I noticed that at many times along the path of my life,
Especially at the very lowest and saddest times,
There was only one set of footprints.

This really troubled me, so I asked the Lord about it.
"Lord, you said once I decided to follow You,
You'd walk with me all the way.
But I noticed that during the saddest and most
Troublesome times of my life,
There was only one set of footprints.

I don't understand why, when I needed You the most,
You would leave me."

He whispered, "My precious child, I love you and
Will never leave you,
Never, ever, during your trials and testings.
When you saw only one set of footprints,
It was then that I carried you."

Without a doubt, God has carried my family. I've seen the
evidence.

Some Final Words

Today I am blessed beyond words. My children and I are living a fulfilled, simple, small-town life and I couldn't be happier. God took me through the valley so I could come out stronger than I ever imagined. Through the storms, I learned to lean on Him and on the peaks, I learned to thank Him.

Writing this book was my healing. It may have taken me years to finally put it to paper, but it also took me years to scratch the surface of grief. If this book can help someone who has suffered a loss, or someone contemplating suicide or help someone identify the signs of someone in need of help, then it's served its purpose. I've learned that people gravitate towards similar situations. Hearing another tragic story might not take your pain away, but it can aid in your healing journey.

About the Author

In her own words:

I am a normal person who grew up in a small town in central Illinois, raised by two industrious parents who taught me that faith, patience, contentment and diligence are the core to life. I'm not only your typical *basketball mom*, I'm also a baseball, softball, track, volleyball and cheer mom. My goals in life are simple: raising my four happy, healthy children well, live each day to its fullest and love with all that I have. The extraordinary situation I faced in 2011 came with many challenges, but I was constantly reminded that God's love never fails.

Casey Powell is also a successful fitness club owner and health and wellness guru. She started her fitness club in 2008 after working in publishing for nine years. She is a Certified John Maxwell Speaker, Coach and Trainer with The John Maxwell Team.

Speaking and Coaching Info

Casey Powell is available for interviews and speaking opportunities. Some of her speaking topics include her testimony and book, plus:

Believe in Yourself
God has a plan for your life
Inspiring women and helping them find their value
Overcoming tragedy
Health and Fitness

Connect with Casey Powell:

www.CaseyPowellAuthor.com
www.facebook.com/casey.powelltrainer
Instagram: caseyjoell_
Twitter: @caseyjoellp

The National Suicide Prevention Lifeline is a national network of local crisis centers providing free and confidential emotional support to people in suicidal crisis or emotional distress 24 hours a day, 7 days a week.

National Suicide Prevention Lifeline
Call 1-800-273-8255
Available 24 hours everyday

Abandoned but Not Crushed is proudly published by:

Creative Force Press

www.CreativeForcePress.com

Do You Have a Book in You?